NEW TESTAMENT THEOLOGY IN DIALOGUE

Books by James D. G. Dunn
published by The Westminster Press

The Evidence for Jesus

*Christology in the Making: A New Testament Inquiry Into the Origins
of the Doctrine of the Incarnation*

*Unity and Diversity in the New Testament: An Inquiry Into the
Character of Earliest Christianity*

Baptism in the Holy Spirit

*Jesus and the Spirit: A Study of the Religious and Charismatic
Experience of Jesus and the First Christians as Reflected in
the New Testament*

NEW TESTAMENT THEOLOGY IN DIALOGUE

Christology and Ministry

James D. G. Dunn
and James P. Mackey

The Westminster Press
Philadelphia

This book was first published in Great Britain in 1987 by SPCK, as part of the series *Biblical Foundations in Theology,* edited by James D. G. Dunn and James P. Mackey.

First American edition

Published by The Westminster Press®
Philadelphia, Pennsylvania

PRINTED IN THE UNITED STATES OF AMERICA
2   4   6   8   9   7   5   3   1

Library of Congress Cataloging-in-Publication Data

Dunn, James D. G., 1939–
New Testament theology in dialogue.

Bibliography: p.
Includes index.
1. Bible. N.T.—Theology. 2. Theology, Doctrinal.
I. Mackey, James Patrick. II. Title.
BS2397.D84 1987   230'.01   87-29592
ISBN 0-664-25020-3

Contents

Preface

This volume takes the form of a simple dialogue. The New Testament scholar first writes about the task of New Testament theology, with a particular eye to changes in our historical consciousness, or what are more professionally called the 'horizons' of the writers and their subsequent interpreters (ch. 1). The systematician then responds with a quite similar account of the task of systematic or dogmatic theology, as it is called (ch. 2). Next, the Scripture scholar takes some themes from New Testament Christologies in order to illustrate more concretely the problems of the relationships, both actual and desirable, between the relevant New Testament texts and subsequent christological dogma (ch. 3). The systematician responds by placing a traditional Christology within its contemporary context in order thereby to open up some prospects of a new view of the Scriptures; a mirror image of the previous chapter, as it were (ch. 4). This process is then repeated by taking another concrete example, an example this time on which Christian Churches disagree rather than one on which they agree: Christian ministry. But the systematician writes first on this occasion (ch. 5) and the New Testament scholar responds (ch. 6).

That is how the dialogue was actually conducted, and the results are offered to the reader. No attempt was made to predetermine the shape or content of opening chapter and responding chapter in each of the three 'pairs' of chapters which constitute the dialogue—nothing beyond the necessary initial agreement on the general topic on which we would engage in dialogue. The conclusion, which we jointly composed as a short epilogue, merely draws attention to what happened in the course of the dialogue itself. But the dialogue's the thing, and on the reader's evaluation of its content will stand or fall his or her first assessment of the worth of the kind of exercise which subsequent volumes in the series aim to carry forward into central areas of Christian theological concern.

NEW TESTAMENT THEOLOGY IN DIALOGUE

1

The Task of New Testament Theology

1 WHAT IS THE NEW TESTAMENT?

The immediate subject matter of New Testament theology is obviously the New Testament. But what is the New Testament? The nature of the discipline is bound to be determined in large measure at least by the character of the subject matter. Yet all too often the question is not asked. The answer is simply taken for granted. The question, after all, is a beginner's question, and by the time we are ready to tackle the subject of New Testament theology we have left such elementary matters far behind us. But on this occasion at least we must pause and be prepared to begin by asking the naively fundamental question. For if the task is, in large part, determined by its subject matter, we must have a clear grasp of the dimensions of that subject matter. Otherwise we may end up charting only the Atlantic and not the Pacific as well, only the land and not the sea.

I normally begin my final year course on New Testament theology by asking this question. After the initial surprise the class's scatter of answers can usually be grouped round two aspects or perspectives:

(a) The New Testament is a collection of *historical documents* – in fact, most of the Christian writings from the first century of our era. As such they are invaluable source documents for any study of the beginnings of Christianity. Almost all our knowledge regarding Jesus and the initial spread of Christianity derives directly from them. Without them we would lose all possibility of direct access to these foundational events.

(b) The New Testament is also *Scripture*. The New Testament writings have been regarded by the Christian Churches as their primary authority down through the centuries, and still are today. Since the earliest centuries the New Testament documents have functioned as 'canon', that is, as rule or yardstick or norm for faith and life. They belong to the class of sacred writings. For generations of Christians they have been heard to speak as the word of God written.

As we shall soon see, there are controversial features about both these ways of regarding the New Testament. But that should not cause us to blank out one or other aspect from the start. To do so would reduce our problems, but would not help in their solution. For unless we begin by acknowledging this twofold historic character of the New Testament documents we will run the risk of ignoring dimensions of our subject matter and so of undermining our task from the outset.

2   WHAT IS NEW TESTAMENT THEOLOGY?

With this preliminary answer to our first question we can go on to our second: What is New Testament theology? Of course we cannot expect a complete or final answer right away. A good deal more clarification and discussion will be necessary before we can hope for that. But it is worth attempting a first approximation to an answer at this stage since that will provide the parameters for the rest of our discussion, or the broad outline which we will hope to fill out as we proceed.

Unfortunately even at this stage we find ourselves caught in a fundamental conflict. The disagreement arises from the two answers given to our first question. For, as we would expect, different views of New Testament theology arise out of the different ways of regarding the New Testament.

(a) For some, New Testament theology is a purely *descriptive* exercise. It is the task of the historian, not of the theologian. Its concern is to lay out the history of early Christian religion and theology. Its object is not to derive observations of continuing theological significance from these writings, but simply to describe the theologies of the New Testament writers, what was believed, thought, taught, hoped, required and striven for in the earliest period of Christianity. Wrede and Stendahl provide classic statements of this understanding of New Testament theology.[1]

(b) For others, New Testament theology will inevitably have a *prescriptive* role in the larger discipline of Christian or dogmatic theology. This arises not simply from a dogma of canonical authority, but from the *fact* of canonical authority. By this I mean the fact that the New Testament has always determined the character and emphases of all subsequent Christian theology in greater or less degree. Even those theologians who have denied the dogma of canonical authority have found it necessary to appeal to the content of the New Testament (Jesus, Paul, John, etc.) to justify their own theological reconstructions. The fact is that the New Testament writings have served as a crucial determinant for the whole of Christian theology. From this perspective, then, the subject matter of New Testament theology is not simply first-century ideas of antiquarian interest but the convictions and experiences which came to expression in the New Testament writings and which can still speak directly to contemporary Christian concerns. New Testament theology means not merely describing the theology of the New Testament but doing theology through the New Testament. The classic response to Wrede at this point is Schlatter.[2]

It would be all too easy to develop these two perspectives as polar alternatives, to save ourselves further trouble by simply labelling them respectively 'liberal' and 'conservative'. That done, we could then each retreat safely into our own theological and ecclesiastical traditions and either ignore the other or snipe away at the other's exposed flanks. The more demanding task is to recognize that there is truth, or at least potential truth in both ways of viewing New Testament theology, and to attempt some kind of rapprochement or positive interaction between them. It is this harder task we attempt to outline here.

3 NEW TESTAMENT THEOLOGY AS A DIALOGUE

The most hopeful way forward is to begin a dialogue between these two different perspectives on New Testament theology. In larger terms that will involve a dialogue between past and present, between first century and twentieth century, between the standpoints of the New Testament writers and their readers on the one hand, and that of the modern exegete on the other.

The descriptive task of New Testament theology requires us to recognize that the New Testament belongs to the first century, with all that that involves (a subject to which we must return). But we cannot get far in the dialogue until we as exegetes also recognize that we ourselves belong to the twentieth century, with all that *that* involves. Apart from anything else, the understanding we bring to the task of exegesis has been shaped by our upbringing and education, by our inherited culture and traditions – including our own theological tradition in its particular distinctiveness.

To cite a few examples: when a British student first comes across the word 'kingdom' in the biblical writings, his understanding is bound to be influenced by the fact that he belongs to the United Kingdom, that his country is a monarchy with an imperial past. His history as a Briton will give shape and content to that word. Or again, his initial understanding of the word 'law' may be influenced by the issue of 'law and order' or by his Reformation heritage. No one is surprised when Roman Catholic and Protestant exegetes come to different conclusions, for everyone knows that they have come to the text from different starting points.

This is the point of Bultmann's question: Is presuppositionless exegesis possible?[3] His answer is clear and obvious: No! Presuppositionless exegesis is an impossibility. We *all*, whoever we are, bring to the text our own 'pre-understanding' – our pre-understanding not just of what its words mean but also of what we expect it to say. To change the metaphor: what we see in a text is limited by the horizon of our own understanding; when we read the text we see only what lies within the horizon which bounds our understanding.

Consequently, a crucial part of the dialogue of New Testament theology is to recognize *that* we have presuppositions, *that* we have horizons – or more precisely, to recognize that our perception will be limited by our presuppositions, our vision limited by our horizons. And to recognize this not simply as a first step which can then be left behind, but to recognize that it will always be true. Our perception of what is there in the text will always be shaped by the language or experience 'bank' from which we draw to 'cash' the words and phrases read. Our understanding will always be limited by our horizons however much these horizons may have expanded in the meantime. If initially we cannot recognize *what* the limits of our horizons are, at least we can recognize *that* they are limited.

And thus we will begin to realize that a sharp antithesis between the alternatives posed above (descriptive versus prescriptive) is somewhat unrealistic. Even the descriptive exercise cannot escape a significant input from the exegete's own viewpoint. That is to say, whether we like it or not, some element of dialogue is essential, if only because it is unavoidable. Better then to engage in the dialogue in positive mood rather than to waste time wishing it could be otherwise.

But is 'dialogue' the right word? For many the alternative to 'scientific objectivity' is the despair of the 'hermeneutical circle'. If we see only what we are able to see from our twentieth-century perspective, or through our Protestant or Catholic spectacles, then are we not simply staring in a sequence of mirrors? If the starting point determines what we find, if the presuppositions determine the conclusions, are we not simply going round in circles? We find what *we* are looking for, answers to *our* questions, and, surprise, surprise, the answers as a rule tend to support our presuppositions. The 'hermeneutical circle' looks to be too much like one of those children's trains at a fun fair, going round and round and round always on the same track, and never getting anywhere. Can we escape?

Yes! The simple answer is that we can correct or improve our pre-understanding. We can broaden our horizons. For example, although a British student begins his New Testament study with a particular idea of what a 'kingdom' is, there is sufficient evidence of the way in which the Aramaic equivalent was used in the first century for him to develop a new understanding of the word, one more informed by the first-century material and less by his twentieth-century heritage. Or again, someone may come to his study of the New Testament with the presupposition of what the 'gospel' says, that evangelistic preaching should always speak of repentance for sins and of God's provision of atonement for sins on the cross. Such a person can check whether this was always so within the New Testament writings. And when he recognizes that Paul hardly speaks of repentance and John never, and that the evangelistic sermons in Acts never present the cross as an act of atonement, he may well find it necessary to redefine his understanding of how the gospel may be preached.

In other words, there is no need for us to keep going round in a circle. We can alter our perspective, re-focus our questions. The circle, if you like, can become more like a spiral; and in pursuing the line of questioning we may hope to find ourselves spiralling in towards the centre.

'Dialogue', however, is the more appropriate metaphor. Our initial questioning should lead to some clearer understanding of the subject matter and to some correction of our initial view-point. This in turn should enable us to pose the question afresh, or to pose the original question more sharply.

At the same time we may well find that the New Testament writings do not merely answer back to our questions. The New Testament may put *us* in question. And may do so so radically that conversion is the only answer possible for us. So Francis of Assisi found with regard to the words of Jesus: 'Sell all that you have and distribute to the poor, and you will have treasure in heaven' (Luke 18.22). Words which he had no doubt heard before now came to him as the word of God and called for total assent. The Reformation's insistence on 'Scripture alone' is an expression of the same experience repeated many times over, when the words of Scripture were heard to speak in a way which challenged generally accepted presuppositions and practices. Or we might reflect on why it is that Liberation theology has arisen in Latin America. For Liberation theology is itself an expression of this same dialogue – where questions have been posed to traditional authorities (including Scripture) by the conditions in these countries, to be met by even sharper questions posed in turn by an important strand of biblical teaching.

I have expressed the dialogue in terms of past and present,

first century and twentieth century addressing each other. There are, of course, other aspects of the dialogue, which would require fuller exploration in a more extended treatment. Here I need merely mention some of them. In particular, the dialogue between old revelation and new, that is, between what has previously been regarded as carrying divine authority and what now claims to be revelation, even though it clashes with the old. Alternatively expressed, the dialogue between tradition and Spirit, between the conservative force of tradition and institution and the liberating experience of a renewal which breaks through the established guidelines. Or again, the dialogue in which many students find themselves caught up, between faith and critical study, where the questioning which orders faith into fundamentals and more ambiguous matters of secondary importance can be very painful. But to explore such as these would take us too far from the present point.

More to the point and of crucial importance is to realize that *this dialogue has already begun in the New Testament itself.* Christianity began as such a dialogue – a dialogue between its Jewish past and the new beginning in Jesus, between Jewish tradition and present Spirit, between old revelation and new. The fundamental dynamic of the New Testament writings is the issue of whether this newly given faith in Christ is simply part of, continuous with, or a departure from the old revelation in Old Testament and Israel. The best example of a phrase which contains the dialogue within itself is 'the people of God'. Who are they? Israel, the seed of Abraham, the Jews, the Christians, only the Jews who believe in Jesus, ...? (Not to mention the Arabs.) Here at least the dialogue of New Testament theology will not cease so long as that question has no clear or agreed answer.

In short, New Testament theology is a dialogue because any twentieth-century attempt to inquire into first-century writings is bound to be a dialogue, because in engaging the New Testament writings with serious theological concerns we frequently find our questions being clarified and ourselves being put in question, and because the New Testament itself is a product of that dialogue, a dialogue in particular between the first Christians and their Jewish heritage.

4 THE PROBLEMS OF NEW TESTAMENT THEOLOGY

So far we have spoken of the dialogue with the New Testament as though the New Testament was a single entity. But in the dialogue of New Testament theology does the New Testament speak with one voice? Whether in descriptive or prescriptive terms, can we speak of the theology of the New Testament? As soon as we ask the question we become aware that it introduces us to a nest of problems.

(a) *Fragmentary sources*. Do the New Testament documents give us a complete testimony of first-century Christianity? The answer is obviously, No! Our sources are incomplete. We do not have all that Jesus said and did (cf. John 20.30). We do not have all the letters written by the first apostles (several of Paul's have not been preserved).

The gaps in our knowledge are enormous. Only Paul's letters were assuredly written within the first Christian generation (before, say, AD 65). What about other apostles and the churches they were involved with? The Acts of the Apostles seems chiefly intent on describing how Paul took the gospel to Rome. What about Alexandria, second largest city of the Roman Empire? What about Antioch (third largest city) after Paul moved the centre of his operations elsewhere?

Few if any of the New Testament writings can be called 'systematic'. All are in greater or less degree occasional: they contain particular emphases because they were addressed to particular situations. What about other emphases? No doubt they were present in the earliest congregations, but because they created no problems nothing has been written about them. In other words, there is an element of the accidental in the composition of our New Testament.

On the other hand, the fact remains that it was just these documents which were preserved. We may presume that they were preserved precisely because their significance for faith was recognized as going beyond the immediate situation which occasioned them. Others were allowed to disappear from view because they were not used, because they did not outlast the occasion or need for which they were written. But these were preserved as having more than temporary importance and their later acceptance as canon was in most cases simply an acknowledgement of the authority they had been increasingly accorded from the first. So however accidental and occasional the New Testament documents were in composition, their significance extended beyond the accidental and occasional from the beginning.

Once again, clearly, we are back with the basic tension between a strictly historical view (2a), which sees the New Testament simply as a sequence of occasional statements, and what we might call a more theological view (2b), which sees these documents as preserved because they were from the first perceived to have an authority which outlived the occasion for which they were written.

(h) *Diversity*. Do the biblical writings speak with a single voice, present a wholly consistent testimony? The immediate answer must again be, No! We have, for example, the differences between Old and New Testaments, illustrated in the transformation of the covenant with Israel into a universal covenant, of the Jewish messianic hope into faith in Christ Jesus, of the Sabbath into Sunday, not to mention the abandonment of such key features of Old Testament law as circumcision, sacrifice and food laws. The problem is that of retaining the Old Testament as *Christian Scripture* within the canon of the Christian Bible. The more we wish to speak of a biblical theology (as distinct from a merely New Testament theology) the more serious the problem. For all the very important and indeed fundamental continuities between Old Testament and New, we cannot ignore the problem of *dis*continuities between the two Testaments. The dialogue with which the New Testament writers as a whole were engaged has its own share of discords and disagreements.

There is also the problem of diversity *within* the New Testament. For example, between Jesus and Paul, where the gospel *of* Jesus has become the gospel *about* Jesus. Or between the Synoptic Gospels and John's Gospel in their remarkably different portrayals of Jesus, particularly so far as his self-testimony is concerned. Or between Matthew and Mark in their presentations of Jesus and the law, with the former able to

present Jesus as quite conservative with regard to the law (as in
Matt. 5.17–20), while the latter shows him abandoning key
commandments of Moses (as in Mark 7.19). Or between Paul
and James on faith and works and in their interpretation of
Abraham's faith (Rom. 3.27–4.25; Jas. 2.18–26). Or regarding
the hope of the Kingdom and of Jesus' coming (again) – realized,
imminent, or yet distant? Or between tradition and redaction:
where we can often detect traditions behind and common to
Synoptics, John and Paul, can we also detect correction of or
alteration to that tradition? All these are examples and evidence
of the fact that the New Testament writings are themselves
caught up in and expressions of the same dialogue – the dialogue
between an individual in his particular historical situation and
a message or faith which transcends that particularity and which
relates to different individuals in different ways.

From the perspective of the later exegete these also point up
the tension between the historical and the theological. On the
one hand, the view which sees the New Testament writings
simply as 'frozen traditions', like a river which a photographer
happens to have 'snapped' at certain points while in motion (cf.
the different 'snaps' of the Christian congregation at Corinth in
1 Corinthians, 2 Corinthians and 1 Clement). A year later here,
a year later there, and the picture would have been different. On
a strictly historical view these frozen traditions can have no
greater value or authority than others *not* snapped. On the other
hand, the more theological view which values the diversity of
the New Testament writings precisely because it shows how
Christianity took shape in different situations with different
formulations of the gospel. To be able to show how faith developed within the New Testament to meet different challenges
can provide an important pointer to the character and expression
of faith today.

(c) *Unity.* In all this diversity is there a centre, a unifying
theme? The very fact that Christianity remained a coherent
movement despite such diversity indicates that there must have
been a centripetal force to counter the centrifugal tendencies of
this diversity. But what was it? The more diverse the theologies
within the New Testament in their particularity, the more important is it to grasp the theological unity which nevertheless
holds them together.

Various answers have been offered to this question, even when it had not been explicitly formulated as a question. For example, within German Protestant scholarship Bultmann in effect argued that the kerygma was the centre.[4] Among his pupils Käsemann on the one hand insisted on the more traditional Lutheran stance that justification by faith was the unifying theme, 'the canon within the canon'.[5] While Braun proposed the more radical alternative that the real unifying thread was the New Testament writers' view of man.[6] In older debates, the Liberal Protestants in the second half of the nineteenth century in effect maintained that Jesus himself, or as we would now say, the historical Jesus, stood alone at the centre of Christianity as it should be. While in the eyes of most Protestants, the effectual unifying element for Roman Catholics is the Church, or more precisely the magisterium.

Here again we must seek to prevent the dialogue breaking down, to avoid the danger of unnecessary polarization. On the one hand, there is the danger of treating the New Testament simply as a source book for doctrine, as though it consisted solely of dogmatic pronouncements. Wrede made a still valuable critique of that approach.[7] And though 'theology' inevitably finds its characteristic expression in doctrine, the task of analysing such theology must necessarily involve an appreciation of how such statements achieve formulation, an appreciation of the dialogue which produces the doctrine. Moreover, the process of doing theology in dialogue with the New Testament involves all the sensitivities to first- and twentieth-century contexts about which we spoke earlier and without which the theologizing becomes a dialogue of the deaf.

On the other hand, there is the danger of adopting what some like to call a 'strictly historical' approach to the New Testament, which sees the New Testament documents simply as an interesting but fragmentary account of earliest Christian religion and in effect as nothing more. In bracketing out the issue of unity or centre as improper or unresolvable such an approach methodologically excludes the possibility that the whole might be greater than the sum of its parts. In ruling out of court as unassessable the truth claims which actually played the most decisive role in establishing Christianity such an approach stifles the dialogue before it has started and reduces the role of the New Testament theologian to that of the historical taxidermist.

In this area the objectives and methods of Schlatter provide a still valuable model and inspiration.[8]

In short, if New Testament theology is to be a dialogue it must strive to maintain itself as a dialogue. It must neither ignore the fragmentary and accidental character of the New Testament writings, nor reduce their significance to the merely occasional. It must give full ear to the diversity contained within these documents and not impose a unity which artificially harmonizes the diversity or excludes some of the differences from the dialogue. But neither must it allow the diversity to obscure the gravitational force which holds all these scattered planets in orbit round the same sun, or to reduce that unifying force to some numbered sequence of dogmatic statements. To enter sensitively into the New Testament is to become aware that it is the product of a living process of faith expressed in a range of diverse situations. To engage in dialogue with it is to appreciate that living process for oneself and to participate in it, sensitive to all the factors which were part of that dialogue from the first.

5   THE CHALLENGE OF NEW TESTAMENT THEOLOGY

How then is the task of New Testament theology to be undertaken? Two words have played an important role in previous attempts to sketch it out, and, properly defined, they still provide guidelines of crucial importance.

(a) *Historical*. The word has so far been used to describe one dimension of the dialogue. We have also noted that the word can be used with a more polarized or negative force – merely historical, or 'strictly historical'. But in any statement of New Testament theology as dialogue the word 'historical' (or its synonym) cannot be avoided. This is simply because the New Testament documents, whatever else they may be, are historical data. They were written in the first century (though one or two may be later) by individuals living in the first century for people living in the first century. However else they are to be understood, therefore, they must be understood in terms of the first century, from within the first century, as it were.

The first aim of New Testament theology must therefore be to set oneself as fully and as sympathetically as possible into the historical context of each New Testament writing, to hear as far as possible as the first readers heard. Only so will there be even the possibility of a real dialogue. Only if we are resolved to let the New Testament writers speak in their own terms, to determine their own priorities and emphases, only then can talk of a dialogue have any meaning. The tendency which we must always be on our guard against is the unconscious imposition of our own meanings and categories on their language.

By historical context I mean both broader context and particular context.

(i) The *broader context* is the context of the culture within which the document was written. The New Testament exegete or theologian cannot begin to do his job properly unless he is sensitive to the fact that the text's language and idiom will inevitably have been determined by and be an expression of broad cultural influences of the time. This is not simply a matter of using concordance and lexicon (what is sometimes called the grammatico-historical method). It is much more a matter of being familiar with the milieu, the attitudes and 'atmosphere' of the times – of being able to recognize, for example, allusions not only to the Old Testament but also to current philosophical and popular beliefs.

To take a modern parallel: a student of literature written in Britain in the late '50s or early '60s of this century might well come across several occurrences of the phrases, 'You've never had it so good', and 'wind of change'. He could not begin to appreciate their force unless he was keenly aware that both phrases had been coined by Prime Minister Harold Macmillan, and that almost certainly their use would carry overtones accordingly. In the same way a student of the New Testament letter to the Hebrews will not get very far in his attempt to hear and understand that letter unless he appreciates that it works with a sophisticated combination of Hellenistic world view (found also in the Alexandrian Jewish philosopher Philo) and Hebraic eschatology.

To put the same point another way, it means being able to recognize what the New Testament writer has been able to take for granted, what does not need to be said, because, of course, 'everyone knows that'. He must be conscious of the degree to which language is only one and only a partial expression of any social world in which individuals live and communicate. To take another modern parallel: any student at a college or university will soon fall into a pattern of conversation, of abbreviations and allusions and jargon words, which will be perfectly meaningful to fellow-students, but mystifying and obscure to others. So within the New Testament, we have no explanation of first-century cosmology, or exposition of Jewish monotheism. We can only work out the New Testament writers' views of the world and understanding of God by listening to what they say and what they do not need to say within the context of first-century Jewish and Hellenistic thought as attested by literature, papyrus documents, inscriptions and archaeological evidence.

For the committed New Testament theologian there is no escape here. He simply must familiarize himself with the broad historical context of which these writings are a part – the history, politics and social conditions of the times, the thought patterns, customs and symbols which they took for granted. That is a tall order, of course. But the alternative, be it said once again, is that the dialogue never begins, or it becomes a pseudo-dialogue, where the New Testament writing functions more like a ventriloquist's dummy, only able to say what its dialogue partner puts into its mouth.

(ii) The *particular context* is the context of the particular situation being addressed. To what extent were the New Testament writers speaking to *specific* situations? It seems to be a fair working assumption that they were not composing 'in the air' but with a view to the needs of some congregation(s). To what extent then were the language and emphases of each writer determined by the needs and situation addressed?

The answer is clear enough in the case of most of Paul's letters. In particular, it is beyond dispute that 1 Corinthians was written because there were a variety of problems troubling the infant congregation in Corinth. As has often been noted, our knowledge of the role and importance of the Lord's Supper in the first Gentile congregations is dependent almost entirely on the 'accidental' fact that there was serious abuse of the common meal at Corinth. What is less appreciated is that since the particular points and emphases Paul makes were addressed to that abuse, we today will not be able to appreciate their full force without a clear idea of what the abuse consisted in. The point has been more readily taken with regard to Paul's counsel earlier in the same letter that in praying or prophesying women should wear a covering on their heads. Few Christian women today feel bound by that counsel since it is generally appreciated that this particular instruction was determined by the social conventions relating to women in first-century Corinth and therefore is of limited applicability.

To take another example. Paul's letter to the Christians in Rome has traditionally been regarded as much less tied to a particular situation, in which case our understanding of it will be less dependent on our knowledge of that situation. But in recent years it has come to be recognized more and more that here too is a letter which arises out of a particular phase in Paul's mission and whose theology reflects that stage in his thinking. Even with Romans, therefore, it will be necessary to inquire into the particular context in Paul's work and thought if we are to appreciate all the various nuances and overtones in the letter.

What about the other New Testament writings? Is the Gospel of John quite so timeless as it has often seemed? Or do we need here too to become aware of particular tendencies and tensions in the Christian assemblies to which the Fourth Evangelist belonged, or was writing to, before we can properly tune in to the message he intended his readers to hear? What about Acts? A history of Christian beginnings, yes indeed. But a history with a purpose or a bias, like all histories. So that if we miss the purpose or misconceive the bias we read the text with blinkers, unaware of all that is going on in the text.

What of Jesus' words themselves? Were they not addressed to particular individuals, often making a point specific to that individual? Without some appreciation of that particular context the words will be open to misunderstanding. It is true that in recording many of these words the Evangelists have transposed them into different contexts and shaped them with a view to their own circumstances. But that is simply to say that many of Jesus' words were adaptable to different contexts and lent themselves to being re-used and variously grouped for various purposes. It does not exempt us from the need to inquire after context and purpose, except that in the case of the Gospels themselves the immediate context and purpose is that of the Evangelists.

There can be no escape then from the task of careful historical exegesis. In particular, we must beware of abusing the benefit of hindsight or the privilege of being able to set these writings within a much broader horizon than was visible to the writers themselves. Our evidence may be fragmentary for the first century Greco-Roman world as a whole. But at least we can set it all out before us. We can take note of what was happening in Rome and in Jerusalem at the same time, in a way that was quite impossible then. We can trace large scale patterns and slow moving cultural transformations of which those active in only one part would hardly have been aware. We can see now how certain tendencies developed into gnostic sects on the one hand or into catholic Christianity on the other. The danger of the hindsight perspective or of too broad horizons is that we not only see the end from the beginning, but we also see the end in the beginning. We too readily assume that such developments were inevitable and that the writers involved at the earlier stages of the development must have been somehow aware of it and intended that it should be so. A properly historical exegesis will ever recall how limited a particular author's horizon must have been and seek to respect that limitation when enquiring what the author intended to say and what his first readers heard him say.

The challenge then is to locate ourselves as firmly as possible within the historical context of the document under study, both the broader context of the culture and the time and the particular context which called forth the writing or to which it was addressed.

(b) *Critical*. The word 'critical' often has a negative tone, as though it meant 'looking for some fault in order to condemn'. But of course it can have a much more positive note as well – 'looking for some weakness in order to improve'. Writers often speak of their spouses as their 'best critic'. A teacher should be the typical critic in this sense. The word itself then simply means a readiness to attempt an evaluation of that being examined. Linked with the previous word it is often used to describe the task of the historian – the 'historical critical method'.

As such it need only mean a readiness to question and evaluate all the data that comes before the historian. It has, of course, been used in a still narrower sense to include the criteria by which such an evaluation may proceed – in particular, the presupposition that all events should be explained in terms of a closed sequence of cause and effect. But here it is used in the more neutral sense of readiness to probe, question and evaluate.

(i) The New Testament critic must be critical of the *text* under examination. That is to say, he must be willing to treat the New Testament texts as products of the first century, and as such to analyse them in the same way as he would other historical texts. Such an examination is not antithetical or hostile to their further role as Scripture. For its purpose is to clarify the character of the documents which were to be recognized as Scripture, to cut through any mystique or dogmatic insistence regarding how things must have been, to appreciate so far as possible the impact which they actually had, without ignoring any features which may now raise an eyebrow. To be properly critical is not to ignore or deny any claims to inspiration on the part of the authors. It is rather to gain a clearer understanding of how inspiration worked and what it produced. Within the Church in fact the New Testament critic is simply carrying out the churches' continuing need to 'test the spirits', to evaluate and assess whatever claims to speak here and now with authoritative voice as the word of God.

New Testament criticism has a number of dimensions. For example, it involves finding the best text of the New Testament. The textual critic aims to get as near to the original text as possible. That means examining all variant readings – that is, all readings which have some claim to be the original reading. Evaluation and assessment of their respective claims is an inescapable part of the textual critic's task. Any student of the New Testament must be aware of this dimension of his task, even if he has no Greek, since then he will be confronted with a variety of translations. But so far as the Greek text is concerned the hard work has already been done by several generations of dedicated textual critics and the text of the New Testament is widely agreed even though numerous minor uncertainties remain.

New Testament criticism also involves recognizing such features of the text as Mark's poor Greek and Paul's confused syntax. Again this is not to criticize (= find fault with) the Holy Spirit! It is simply to acknowledge that if the Spirit is the author of these documents then the Spirit used poor Greek and confused syntax! If this too can be an aspect of inspired speech and canonical Scripture we should not shut our eyes or ears to it.

The New Testament critic will also want to penetrate below the surface of the text, to recognize the use of earlier traditions. How a writer has made use of the material available to him may tell us much about his purpose and meaning. This dimension of New Testament criticism has been particularly important in the Gospels – what sources they used, written or oral; how the material came to them, in small units or larger blocks; how and why that material took the forms it did; how and why the one who stamped his authorship on the Gospel used that material as he did. Without such critical inquiry we cannot hope to make sense of the differences between the Synoptic Gospels and John's Gospel. With such inquiry we can hope to appreciate more fully the impact of Jesus' words and deeds both immediately and during the generation before the first Gospel was written.

To take but one other example: to be properly critical means readiness to recognize tensions within the New Testament – tensions within a text, as when John 14.31 seems to bring Jesus' teaching to an end only for it to carry on for two more chapters; or tensions between texts, such as were outlined above in 4b. Not least it means readiness to cope with tension between the text and our own assumptions – which brings us to our last point.

(ii) The New Testament critic must be critical of *himself*. This means, basically, being willing to recognize the *possibility* that the text will speak with a different voice and message from what he had presupposed – being willing to take this seriously as a methodological possibility. So if the New Testament critic is inclined to come to the text from a 'strictly historical' viewpoint, or using the historical critical method in the narrower sense, he must be open to the possibility that the texts do have an extra dimension, whether described in terms of inspiration, revelation or word of God. To be properly critical he must be critical of his own viewpoint, of his historical critical method. If, on the other hand, his inclination is to come to Scripture with an already established pattern of faith, he must be open to the possibility that that pattern is inadequately grounded in the text, that exegesis may point to conclusions which call important aspects of that faith in question.

In other words, an essential characteristic of the New Testament critic (as of any critic) is *openmindedness* – a willingness to ask questions and to follow through the answers and their corollaries. Openmindedness is not the same as empty mindedness, though some teachers have made the mistake of confusing them. Empty mindedness asks for the impossibility of offering the mind as a blank sheet, on which new truths may be imprinted with pristine freshness. Openmindedness recognizes that presuppositionless inquiry is impossible, takes into account that the New Testament critic will approach his task with some sort of faith. Openmindedness is what makes a true dialogue possible – a dialogue between the student of the New Testament, wherever he or she is, and the text itself, whatever it is. An *open* dialogue, which allows *all* questions to be asked, and which is ready to consider all potential answers. An open *dialogue*, which allows answers to react back on the starting point, to criticise the faith which prompted the initial question, to correct or abandon presuppositions which the dialogue shows to be faulty.

For example, what if 2 Peter was *not* written by the apostle Peter? What would that say about 2 Peter? about its canonical status? about the canon? What if Matthew and Mark actually do disagree about Jesus and the law? Is one more 'right' than the other? Or can both be 'right'? What if there is real estrangement and even some antagonism between Paul and the law? What does that tell us about Paul? about the Old Testament in relation to the New? What if, on the other hand, we find that even after all our critical work Jesus does not seem to fit any normal category? if after all rationalization of various miracle stories there still seems to be something more? if the resurrection faith of the first Christians makes no sense without postulating that something had happened to Jesus, 'the resurrection of Jesus'? What if after the most penetrating analysis of a text which sets it firmly in its first-century context it still leaps from the page and addresses us as God's word?

To be properly critical, to be genuinely openminded can make an interesting historical inquiry into a dialogue of discovery, where the discovery is as much about oneself as about the text being questioned.

6   THE TASK OF NEW TESTAMENT THEOLOGY

In the light of all that has been said the task of New Testament theology can be more fully defined.

(a) The task of New Testament theology is to hear what the New Testament author intended his readers to hear, and so to hear that the message of the text helps shape our own theology. (i) The immediate aim then is the aim of exegesis: to understand the text as it was intended to be understood; and to appreciate what it was that the first readers heard which caused them to preserve and treasure this text. Since we have other sources and data from this period, we can hope for a degree of objectivity in our exegesis which enables us to criticize both the text and ourselves and thus for a true dialogue to proceed. A mark of this is the exegete's sense of the strangeness and foreignness of so much of his material – for example, of Jesus the first-century Palestinian eschatological prophet, of Paul in his theological statements about the role of women, of the bizarre nature of apocalyptic imagery. A sense of such strangeness is a good sign since it helps ensure that we are not simply imposing our own meaning on the text.

To express the objective of exegesis in this way is to give high priority to 'author's intention'. In literary critical circles that is a contentious phrase. But in the case of the New Testament writings it is both meaningful and highly relevant, since they were all written with particular purposes in view and these purposes are usually fairly obvious even when not fully explicit. It is more complicated, of course, when an author is drawing on material formulated earlier: exegetical analysis of a text may have to cope with more than one editorial layer – the Fourth Gospel being the most obvious case in point. But nevertheless we can still speak of an author, even with John's Gospel, since in every case it is evident that some individual has stamped the writing with its enduring character.

The importance of insisting on the priority of author's intention as the immediate aim is twofold. In the first place, it prevents the dialogue lapsing into a pseudo-dialogue, where the text is treated without regard for the original context, which informs its original meaning, and in effect has a different context imposed upon it. In the worst of such cases the supposed autonomy of the text is once again little better than the autonomy of the ventriloquist's dummy. In the second place, the author of a text must surely be given first claim to it – it is *his* text. And that means also first claim to determine the meaning of the text. His meaning is *the* meaning. And if other meanings are to be read from the text, they must always be measured against his meaning. The further they are from the meaning he intended, the more open to question are they. In the end of the day, it is the author's intended meaning which must serve as the normative meaning, the check against imposing meaning on the text. Only *ex*egesis can prevent *eis*egesis.

(ii) There is more to it however. For we are talking about a dialogue. And a dialogue allows the possibility that as the dialogue develops the tones and emphases will change, agreement will be reached at some points, and fresh issues will arise at others. As different questions are put to the same texts, by different generations in different circumstances, so it will almost certainly be the case that the meaning heard from the text will be different. That is simply to say that *interpretation* will by no means always emerge with the same result as *exegesis*. A classic example is Luther's quest for a quiet conscience and a gracious God. This resulted in an individualistic doctrine of justification by faith which was significantly different from Paul's more corporate vision of Gentiles equally acceptable as Jews within the people of God.

That however does not change the normative force of the author's original meaning. It simply means that interpretation must always be dependent on exegesis, that fresh interpretation must always stay within the bounds set by what is compatible with exegesis. For the dialogue to continue the partners must continue to be themselves, the one belonging to the first century, the other to the twentieth century, and however far from these home bases the dialogue takes them, each must keep firmly in touch throughout. The alternative is the manipulation of the text by the interpreter or the increasing inability of the interpreter to communicate with his own time.

The exciting potential of the dialogue of New Testament theology is that at its best it enables the New Testament theologian both to hear the message of his texts with first-century ears and to explain or re-express that message with twentieth-century lips. It is when the twentieth-century exegete has immersed himself in the historical context of his text and entered sympathetically and critically into its meaning, that he may then hope to find that he himself has become the hermeneutic bridge which spans the centuries and cultures and allows the impact of these writings to be experienced once again twenty centuries later.

(b) All this has been expressed in individual terms, as though it was a task carried out solely by a set of individual exegetes and theologians. To present it thus has been more a matter of convenience than anything else, to keep the description relatively simple and uncomplicated.

However, it is of crucial importance to recall also that the task of theology is a *corporate* one. The New Testament theologian operates within a double context, reflecting the two-sided character of his primary subject matter – the community of scholarship and the community of faith. He is responsible to both – to share his insights and to accept their criticism.

Truth is seldom simple enough to be fully grasped by a single mind. And when that truth is the truth of a particular first-century context and meaning, of whose complexity we cannot now be fully aware, it is of critical importance that different individuals engaging in dialogue with that text from all their different twentieth-century contexts engage also in dialogue with one another. Insights gleaned by different viewpoints and different expertise will provide a stereoscopic view of increased depth which would be impossible for the individual working on his own. Of course, the individual specialist naturally tends to honour his own discipline by attributing as much significance to it as he can in explaining the data under examination – this

applies as much to the theologian as to the psychologist or
sociologist. But such professional pride will almost certainly
lead as often as not to a distorted picture of the whole. The
individual specialist needs to bear in mind his own limited
horizons, and for the sake of truth needs to be open to the fuller
view provided by the diversity of specialisms and to the correction to his own more limited perspective which they make
possible.

The same is true within the community of faith. The New
Testament theologian has a responsibility to the community of
faith to speak the truth as he sees it, to unfold the reality of the
New Testament, its strangeness as historical documentation as
well as its claim on faith as Scripture. And since the meaning
intended by the original author should have normative significance in all matters of interpretation, the New Testament
theologian has the particular responsibility constantly to recall
the community of faith to that meaning and to provide a lead in
the task of doing theology through the New Testament. But his
is only one gift and function within the community of faith. And
if the New Testament theologian exalts his role too highly the
result will again be distortion and imbalance. For theological
truth, like all truth, is many-faceted. And it needs the different
roles and gifts of the Body of Christ to bring that truth out in
its fullness.

Moreover, no claim to make an authoritative pronouncement
has ever been accepted at face value or been regarded as self-
authenticating within the Judaeo-Christian tradition. The
words of prophets were tested to eliminate false prophecy. The
words of Jesus have been subjected to interpretation from the
beginning. The word of God has to be heard as such before it
is obeyed or reckoned worthy of preservation. How much more
then the offering of exegete and teacher, of interpreter and
theologian. To function within the community of faith the New
Testament theologian requires and depends on the evaluation
and assent of the community. The dialogue of New Testament
theology takes place within the community, with all the possibility of correction and sharpened insight which this involves.

(c) This brings us to a further observation. What has been
described so far has been principally the task of the academic or

professional theologian. In relation to the community of faith that task has just been circumscribed and qualified by pointing out that it is only one gift or function within the community of faith, which needs to be evaluated and complemented by other gifts and roles if it is to make its proper contribution to the upbuilding of faith.

But it has to be qualified in at least one other way. For to confine the task of New Testament theology to the professional theologian would be as unjustified and inaccurate as it is to confine theology to the academic world. Of course the professional has a special expertise and calling which is not widely shared within the community of faith. That is why the theologian must be willing to put his historical and critical expertise at the service of the community as a whole, to be one element in the community's theological dialogue, as we have just said. But *anyone* who tries to bring the New Testament writings to bear on his own thought and life and social context is doing New Testament theology, whether he describes it as such or not. And that applies to most if not all members of the Christian churches at some time or other.

To discern an author's meaning, to hear the New Testament properly as Scripture need not by any means depend on a vast apparatus of scholarly expertise. On the contrary, the scholar can often become so caught up in the complexity of his analysis that he loses sight of the meaning clearly intended by the author. The faith that enters the dialogue of New Testament theology uncluttered with details of doubtful disputes can often hear what the text has to say with a freshness and a simplicity which the professional theologian has missed or forgotten. This too is part of the dialogue at a community level.

The point here, however, is that *whoever* engages in New Testament theology must recognize that New Testament theology is a dialogue, involving the same problems as were outlined above, needing the same kind of historical and critical involvement in one degree or other. There is no virtue in simplicity for simplicity's sake, if the truth involved is in fact more complex. The 'ordinary believer' should by no means regard himself as excluded from the dialogue of New Testament theology. But he should recognize that he is subject to the same dangers as the professional theologian – of the dialogue becoming unbalanced, of the bridge of New Testament theology losing its footing in either first or twentieth centuries, or both.

Here again, it needs to be said, the dialogue of New Testament theology is a dialogue within the community of faith. The New Testament theologian can only offer his own insights and interpretations for evaluation by the whole community. To do less is to arrogate claims of truth to oneself. But this applies as much to the 'lay' theologian as to the professional. The community needs to respect expertise where that is present, and to be sensitive to the aspects of the dialogue which the professional can provide. But it has also to encourage all its members to engage in the daily dialogue of New Testament theology, to be open to critical comments from all participants, and to play its own part in evaluating and assessing all claims on its attention Only so can the task of New Testament theology fulfil its proper role.

(d) A final note on the relation between New Testament theology and dogmatic theology, which has been the subject of reflection for two hundred years.[9] From what has been said it will be evident that they are closely related.

On the one hand, they are *not* the same. Apart from anything else, the subject matter of New Testament theology remains restricted by its unceasing reference to the New Testament writings themselves. Dogmatic theology, however, must obviously range wider, to embrace not only historical theology but also themes and issues not raised by or within the New Testament.

On the other hand, New Testament theology is clearly part of dogmatic theology. Since the New Testament itself must be part of the subject matter of dogmatic theology, New Testament theology is in effect a subsection of dogmatic theology. But because of the canonical force of the New Testament it also follows that New Testament theology must exercise some sort of check or control within the wider discipline. Dogmatic theology is a wider dialogue than New Testament theology, but where dogmatic theology relates to issues on which New Testament theology has a say, it follows that New Testament theology must be allowed to play its normative role in that wider dialogue.

NOTES

1   W. Wrede, 'The Task and Methods of "New Testament Theology"', in R. Morgan, *The Nature of New Testament Theology* (London, SCM, 1973) pp. 68–116; K. Stendahl, 'Biblical Theology', *The Interpreter's Dictionary of the Bible* (Nashville, Abingdon, 1962) vol. i pp. 418–32.

2   A. Schlatter, 'The Theology of the New Testament and Dogmatics', in Morgan, *Nature*, pp. 117–66.

3   R. Bultmann, 'Is Exegesis without Presuppositions Possible?', *Existence and Faith* (London, Collins Fontana, 1964) pp. 342–51.

4   R. Bultmann, 'The New Testament and Mythology', in H.-W. Bartsch, *Kerygma and Myth* (London, SPCK, 1953).

5   E. Käsemann, *Das Neue Testament als Kanon* (Göttingen, Vandenhoeck, 1970).

6   H. Braun, 'The Problem of a Theology of the New Testament', *Journal for Theology and the Church* 1 (1965), pp 169–83.

7   Above n 1.

8   Above n 2.

9   See, e.g., H. Boers, *What is New Testament Theology?* (Philadelphia, Fortress, 1979).

2

The Task of Systematic Theology

'New Testament theology is in effect a sub-section of dogmatic theology...Dogmatic theology is a wider dialogue than New Testament theology.' These closing statements from the first chapter form a fine introduction to further inquiry. Indeed, since these statements are so true, many of the themes discussed in the first chapter will find in this chapter a broader relevance and a more extensive illustration. The need to set theologies in their historical and cultural milieux if ever they are to be properly understood, the need to know a good deal about the composers of particular theologies and about the audience or the 'enemies' they had in view; such themes must first be investigated. Only then can the theme so central to this volume, viz., the relationship between New Testament and systematic theology, and in particular the claim that because of the canonical force of the New Testament, New Testament theology must exercise control within the wider discipline, receive any adequate treatment. And then, and only then, it should be possible to return once more to the very basic theme which was sounded or evoked so very frequently in the course of the first chapter: the theme of history and faith, of older times and our day; the question, Are we digging up the past from some form of archaeological interest, preserving and sometimes for this very purpose refurbishing some traditional beliefs in a kind of museum of religions, or is something as important as the deepest or highest of human faith somehow involved in all of this? But first to a more elementary introductory question, similar to the one which opened the first chapter.

1   WHAT IS SYSTEMATIC THEOLOGY?

The confusion of names does not help in answering this question. Systematic theology or dogmatic theology? The former is more frequently preferred these days for a number of reasons, not least of which is the poor impression which the very use of the term 'dogmatic' tends to convey. Christians are uncomfortably aware of the fact that an increasing number of their contemporaries already consider them too dogmatic, in the popular sense of the word, and they are anxious to ameliorate their image. They may be quite unaware of the fact that the use of the phrase 'dogmatic theology' does not in any case much predate the seventeenth century. Yet, in spite of all that, an unbiased understanding of this phrase can offer very substantial clues to the nature of the discipline which it still sometimes names.

'Dogma' is an old Greek word which could mean *either* an order, a statute, a decree *or* the basic positions, the characteristic principles adopted by, say, an individual philosopher or a school of philosophy. And indeed it is this variety of meaning which enables it to name the discipline which we now try to describe. For at the heart of this discipline are the most generally acceptable formulations of the things which Christians believe and, naturally, believe to be true. By formulations I mean didactic, doctrinal, and systematic (hence the other title for the discipline) expositions of Christian beliefs, in contrast to more poetic, literary, artistic expressions of the same belief. This accords with the second meaning above of the old Greek word. But the first meaning is also important, if only because some of the doctrinal formulae worked out in dogmatic theology were in fact adopted and imposed by authoritative bodies in the course of Christian church history, and they then became at least part of creeds or confessions or conciliar or papal definitions of the Christian faith: they took on the stature of decrees for the Churches to which they were issued.

Dogmatic theology is the discipline which arrives at these 'dogmas' either in the more private sense of the doctrinal positions of theologians and schools of theology, or the more public sense of those theological formulations adopted officially in some authoritative form, and it is the discipline which looks at them again and again with a view to explaining and retaining, or revising, or even replacing them. To call it 'systematic theology' is simply to claim that it performs this exercise systematically, with a clear and consistent logic relevant to the exercise itself.

But how does this discipline arrive at 'dogmas'? To what does it look in order to formulate such doctrinal expositions, or indeed in order to explain, revise and replace them? The answer to this question is quite concrete, but like many a concrete thing it can require a fairly complex description. The clue to the answer was given by G. L. Prestige when he said that the Christian faith has been out at interest in the intellectual banks from the very beginning. But the clue will only work for those who realize that from the very beginning the Christian faith has been a 'way', a way of life. Jesus is reputed to have said 'I am the way, and the truth and the life', and it is therefore quite probable that the primordial form of truth for Christians is a kind of life which by God's gracious presence they believe they are enabled to live. Now the most natural expression of a life is a story, and it should therefore come as no surprise that the story was a dominant form in which the early followers of Jesus communicated their faith, the story which told of Jesus' own origins, life, death, and destiny, and of his followers coming together, breaking bread, breaking down walls of division, celebrating God's presence and forgiveness, and the extrapolation from 'the story so far' in order to tell of yet greater things expected both in terrestrial history and beyond the darkness of death.

The New Testament is full of story. So, for instance, is that early creed now known as the Apostles' Creed. But just as human imagination is always accompanied by intellectual reflection, by reflective thinking about the story one is telling or hearing and the image one is fashioning, so from the beginning reflective thought accompanied the Christian stories and the ensuing doctrinal formulae are liberally interspersed with these stories. Paul told the story of the Last Supper in 1 Corinthians 11, but he is soon drawing some very didactic implications for some of his Corinthian converts whose conduct he found far from exemplary; four chapters later he is telling the story of Jesus' resurrection and 'appearances', but his reflection soon leads him to the doctrinal formula that Jesus, the last Adam, became a life-giving spirit. And in general the stories of Jesus' life, death and destiny yield the quasi-credal confession that Jesus is Lord (i.e. divine). Similarly, into a very story-like creed, now known as the Nicene Creed, doctrinal formulae such as 'true God from true God' and the more erudite 'one in substance with the Father' were inserted, the fruits of long theological discussions and of bitter theological battles. In attempting to arrive at its 'dogmas' then, as in every attempt to explain, revise or replace them, the discipline known as dogmatic theology attends to the lives that people live by the spirit of Jesus, the eucharistic lives they live in chapel and market-place, as they take the bread of life with gratitude from God, and break it to give to others in the indomitable hope of more abundant life and grace for all. But since it is, after all, an academic discipline, dogmatic theology attends more nearly to the expression of this life in story, and since it is a Christian academic discipline, erected on the belief that Jesus is the source of this faith-life of his rather erratic followers, it attends most closely to the story of Jesus, and principally to the earliest and most authoritative stories of the New Testament.

The discipline also attends to its own previous formulations. Like many another discipline it can at times become so narcissistic that it seems to attend to little else. Indeed Roman Catholics in particular have often given other Christians to believe that because of their peculiar doctrine of infallibility, those 'dogmas' to which their Church has given highest authority are themselves irreformable and thus absolute starting points for all further reflection. But the best Roman Catholic theologians today reject such implications of this oddly-stated doctrine. They point out that, although the whole Christian community in the world enjoys Jesus' promise that it will not fail (and it is in that sense 'infallible'), no doctrinal formula is in itself irreformable, and all must be critically assessed over and over again against the life of Jesus, still imperfectly detectable in his followers, and against the ritual drama and the story in which that life finds primary expression. For if the case were otherwise, then the formulated 'dogmas' in Christianity, all of them distillations of theologics, would take precedence in the Christian religion over the lives of Christians and the way in which they walk; and that would surely be a distortion of the faith and an unwelcome elevation of the theologian.

The beginnings of Christian systematic theology are probably to be found in the writings of those who from the second century of the Christian era were known as the apologists for the new faith. The impetus to give a reflectively reasoned or doctrinal (i.e. 'teaching') account of the truth one had found in life is, as has just been said, interspersed from the beginning with more prominent imaginative presentations. But it was erected into a separate and distinct task by men like Justin Martyr, who felt that they had to make a full and adequate defence of their new lives to their learned pagan contemporaries, and that they had to make full use for this very purpose of the kind of 'philosophical' treatise which served so well their cultured despisers. The relationship between the new faith and its wider cultural milieu, always at least implicit, now becomes quite explicit by the very nature of the apologists' task. Justin indeed explicitly appeals to his opponents' theology of the divine 'word' and divine sons in making his case for Jesus as the Son of God and the Word incarnate – and this relationship will form the substance of the first theme which we must investigate.

Unfortunately not all of the theological battles of the followers of Jesus were waged with outsiders. The community seems to have been rent from the start by rival interpretations of Jesus, and some of these soon proved entirely incompatible. This 'tearing' became known, after another Greek word, as 'heresy'. And so, once again in the second century AD, the full didactic treatise, the extended reflective argument, is used to answer those believed to be engaged in heresy. Amongst the very earliest treatises on the Christian belief in God as Trinity are works written by Tertullian against Christians now otherwise unknown to us called 'Noetus' and 'Praxeas'. In fact a surprising amount of systematic theology from the third century to the great compendia of theology in the Middle Ages is motivated by the desire for final victory over what are believed to be the systematic presentations of heretical 'dogmas'. Much the same could be said for Christian theology after the Protestant Reformation of the sixteenth century. Only in very recent times do we find substantial numbers of theological works which can be read through without any inkling of sectarian intentionality. The very prominent role of inner-Christian polemics in the development of dogmatic theology is the second of the themes

to be investigated before we can seriously talk about the New
Testament and systematic theology; for, to say the least, theologians of all Christian persuasions quite frequently had other
things on their minds besides that calm and reflective meditation
upon the Bible from which systematic theology could best
benefit.

2   SYSTEMATIC THEOLOGY IN ITS
HISTORICAL AND CULTURAL MILIEUX

It has often been noted that the central Christian doctrines, the
formulations concerning God and Jesus, received their definitive shape before the end of the fifth century AD, and that only
in very recent times has that traditional shape sustained any
serious challenge. Other doctrinal positions, on church, ministry, sacraments, and on the nature of reconciliation, redemption
and final hope, were more fluid and took longer to settle in
generally acceptable moulds; and then these moulds were all
broken open in the great creative eruption of the Protestant
Reformation of the sixteenth century. It is the doctrinal formulations about God and Jesus, therefore, which provide for
Christians the most commonly acceptable examples of the relationship between dogmatic theology and the broader cultural
milieux, but if we are to see that relationship in the case of these
formulations we must look to the prevailing culture in which
these doctrines developed. We deal, as always in Christianity,
with living realities or real life experiences; in this case with an
experienced presence of Jesus as a divine spirit inspiring
people's daily lives, and with an experienced encounter in that
spirit with the immanent creator God whom Jesus called Father,
whose grace is in the sun and the rain and the wheat put to sickle
for each harvest. In the general cultural milieu of the first five
centuries there were other gods in the heavens and on the
earth – money was, no doubt, already one of them – and people's
lives, summarized in their rituals, showed which god was theirs.
The broadest question of the relationship of developing
Christianity to its cultural milieux, therefore, would require a
general comparison of the lives and rituals of Christians 'real'
and 'fake' with the lives and rituals of others. But we are

concerned, mercifully, only with Christian theology, that very much second-level expression of Christian faith, and so what we need for our comparison is the similar second-level expression of the rival religious faiths with which Christians willy-nilly found themselves in contact.

Now it so happens that the kind of religious faith which found the most impressive second-level expression, and which therefore most influenced early Christian theologians, was the religious faith of Platonism. Platonism had by this time absorbed the best religious insights of Aristotle, the Stoa, the Pythagoreans. It is known as Middle Platonism and from the third century onward, because of the great reforming genius of Plotinus, it is named Neoplatonism. Christians had to encounter divinity as a presence of the spirit of Jesus in lives and rituals entangled with, and yet distinguished from, the lives and rituals of the highly religious 'pagans' amongst whom they lived. But they had to work out the 'dogmas' which would express their living faith in formulations entangled with, and yet distinguished from, the formulations which the most erudite of their highly religious 'pagan' contemporaries had evolved. Otherwise they could not have addressed their contemporaries at a theological level, and in any case, most if not all early Christian theologians, whether converts or cradle Christians, used in their theologizing an educational background which was impregnated by 'pagan' theology.

Here we meet one of the commonest and most misleading conceits of the history of Christian theology. It is the insistence that the so-called pagan Greek theology with which these early erudite Christians had to deal was really philosophy as distinct from theology, a product of autonomous human reason rather than an answer to divine revelation, a pulling oneself up by one's own bootstraps; pride, as Augustine put it, rather than the due humility of the fallen creature. In a more modern form the same conceit can be found in Karl Barth's positive phobia about natural theology. For natural theology is contrasted with revealed theology, as faith is with reason and nature with grace, and the thought of these early Platonists is still taken as a classic example of what must on these grounds be rejected at all costs. The conceit in modern times is no doubt supported by the modern break between Christianity and the major figures in

European philosophy who after Hegel came to consider
Christian faith irrational – and it is now to a great extent in
collusion with such a judgment upon Christian faith. But it is,
in both ancient and modern forms, misleading at best. At worst
it reminds one of the acid comment of Marx: 'Theologians
establish two kinds of religion. Every religion which is not their
own is an invention of man, and hence artificial, while their own
comes from God.'[1]

Now it simply must be recognized that there is not now nor
has there ever been a 'natural' theology which could be defined
in contrast to revealed theology. There never has been a theology
which did not itself proclaim its utter dependence upon God's
previous revelation in nature and usually also in history, just as
Christians proclaim the utter dependence of their faith and its
subsequent theologizing on God's revelation in nature and history. Nor is there any point in trying to counter these assertions
by claiming that there are kinds of doctrine or of theological
concept or image which have no parallels in the thought of one's
rivals, and in this way to 'prove' Christianity a revealed religion
in a manner in which those are not. Christians have a doctrine
of the Fall; so had the so-called pagan Greeks. Plato too came
to be considered a quasi-divine being, conceived of no earthly
father, *and* his writings were extant: the *Timaeus*, for instance,
was an authoritative text. But Christians believed in creation out
of nothing; yes, and that doctrine is clearly found in Porphyry's
commentary on the *Timaeus*. Christians evolved a Trinitarian
doctrine of God; so, as we shall see, did the Platonists. And so
on. There is not a single theological category which Christians
use or have used which was not there before them.

Furthermore, Western philosophy down to Hegel was theological at its summit, and therefore it was theological to its very
core. And even after Hegel, when the great systems of secular
humanism emerged, it became obvious to any who were not
blinded by the simplistic dichotomies between faith and reason,
that these also moved at the same depth and with the same
comprehensiveness as theological systems, that they attempted
to account for the whole of reality and the highest of human
aspirations, and that they were therefore in their totalities no
less objects of faith than were their theological alternatives.
Indeed, at their heart and centre they too were 'ways' in which

humankind was invited to walk, and for which human beings have frequently been asked to die. In their case also the philosophy was to the 'way' as in Christianity theology is to the Christian way – the reflective, systematic, 'scientific' exposition of the way. And certainly where one can be asked to die for a way, as happened in Marxism and Nazism, one is dealing in absolutes as obvious as any religious absolutes were ever obvious.

The point of all this rapid comment is to prove that what Christians have always encountered in surrounding cultures are comparable faiths; hitherto, religious faiths; more recently, in addition, faiths which are the powerful secular counterparts to religious faiths. They never did and they do not now encounter 'neutral' philosophies which conveniently leave lying about sets of concepts, elastic in substance, which Christians can simply fill with, and simultaneously shape to, the context of their own living faith. And the point of saying that every theological concept or category which Christians used was there before them is this: to secure the realization that all of these concepts and categories were already filled and shaped by the distinctive life experience of the faiths which had developed the theologies to which they belonged; and they had therefore to be taken as such and enriched or reformed by Christians who wished to operate in the same culture or who had no option but to do so. Only in this way could the distinctively Christian life find expression for all, Christians and others, who shared the same culture.

On the contrary, the more Christians were tempted to think that they could pick up neutral concepts or categories (religiously neutral because they were attributed to reason rather than revelation, to nature rather than grace), the more they ran the risk, and still run the risk, of taking over quite unwittingly great dollops of the distinctive faiths of others and then thinking it was their own. So the overall point of this section is to say that Christians in fact took over more than they realized of other faiths. Sometimes they did so to such a degree as to damage the distinctive experience of their own faith, so much that the challenge of their own distinctive faith was then less accessible either to themselves or to others. It was simply a continuation and an increase of this same insensitivity towards the distinctive faiths, the distinctive lives, and consequently the distinctive myths and theologies of other peoples, when European missionaries carried across the world European concepts and categories, conventions and institutions, and borrowed from these peoples little more than their languages, if they did even borrow these. When they acted in this way, and too often in the past they did act in this way, they were more likely to cause the death of a culture than the genuine spread of a distinctive faith. Then the exclusivism of Christianity too often became a self-fulfilling prophecy, as well as a menace to the divine light which, according to the opening verses of the Fourth Gospel, enlightens *every* man who comes into the world. The only way in which Christians ever could or ever can witness their faith to others in theological form is to learn of the faith of others through shared cultural categories; then they learn their own faith again, as they learn how to enrich or revise these categories, with full respect for them, in order to reveal what is truly distinctive and offer it for free acceptance to those who can take it. Jesus, after all, was a Jew and remains a Jew to this day.

We can but offer as examples here some of the commonest and earliest Christian 'dogmas' about God and Jesus, as we ask how well or ill the early Christian apologists and theologians expressed their religious faith to the learned believers in a Platonic faith. Restrictions of space require that we put the matter far too crudely; but for the sake of brevity let us say that the learned Platonist believer of the first centuries of the Christian era believed that everything good, indeed everything positively describable, came from God and from nothing other than God, and that it came (to be) as a result of God's overflowing goodness; and because of this original fact there was in this creation enough of God's own light and life to lure people back to God who was their true home. The Platonic theology of God, consequently, developed a strong sense of 'binity', and later trinity, within the one being of the divinity. It conceived of the One, the inner being of God which was 'beyond all substance' as Plato had said, and therefore beyond all human knowing. But it also conceived of God as the Light which streamed into the world, as an enlightening thing, a thing intelligible, like word or mind; and, further, as an enlivening, an inspiring thing, like soul or spirit; and these further 'grades' or levels (to borrow a phrase from Tertullian) of divinity-in-outreach could, it thought, be known by human minds, and through these God would finally be reached if only by a final and even more gratuitous gift of light. For these three inner-divine distinctions Plotinus actually used the term *hypostasis*, the very term Eastern Christians later used for each of the Three in their Trinity.

The same Platonic theologian, thinking now about the creation by this unqualifiedly good God, felt something of a deep and insidious dismay at the materiality of things; for to the fact that they were material he naturally attributed such evils as separation and loneliness, change, decay and death. So he tended to see in soul rather than body the likeness of the divine, the image of God; he preferred to talk of saving souls, and leaving bodies to return to the matter from which they came. Plotinus knew that the being of God at that level of its outreach at which it touched its own physical creation, could suffer from change because of the accidental fact – accidental to its own pure nature – of its saving contact with its world. Nevertheless the whole thrust of his religious thought was, as with Platonists generally, towards the heaven of pure spirit, pure divine being and pure immortal soul. The soul-body distinction is very much a Platonic 'dogma'.

We shall take up some concrete examples of Christian 'dogmas' later in this work and ask how biblical they are, or indeed how Christian. But we might pause at this point to ask in a general way how the early Christian theologians managed to infuse into these dominant theological conceptions of that Greek culture their own distinctive beliefs about a God *fully* incarnate, indeed a crucified God. It was so fatally attractive to them to borrow Platonic trinitarian forms, to proclaim that the One was Jesus' Father and that the 'word' or 'nous' of the One was incarnate in Jesus so that the One could in this way be at last definitively known. But in the course of this most obvious and effective use of existing theological concepts, how much of the typical Platonist distinction of soul and body, how much of the underlying Platonic experience of dismay about matter, entered the Christian soul? The main 'dogma' about Jesus which comes from these centuries and still dominates Christian thought today, is of a divine *and* a human nature united in one 'person' or '*hypostasis*'. But the impression has lasted down the centuries of a kind of deep dualism in Jesus. Only his human, bodily part suffered on the cross; his divine nature remained impassible. Further, as in most dualisms, the two 'sides' are rivals. The more we say Jesus is divine in such an atmosphere, the less like us we can imagine him to have been; the more human history proves him to be, the more difficult we find it to continue to believe that he was divine. Where then goes the distinctively Christian conviction that God in Jesus fully entered human history and in so doing took human history with all its suffering and tragedy into the centre of his own very being?

Because of its inevitable insertion in a sequence of historical and cultural milieux systematic theology must forever be critical; critical, of course, in the sense of that word used in the first chapter, viz., willing to assess alleged successes and to admit possible failures, or, as is mostly the case, partial success and partial failure. It must pay the closest and most respectful attention to the religious concepts of the cultures through which it has passed. Often it is only when a Christian has studied Platonic religion carefully and thoroughly for its own sake and for the first time that he or she will ask: but what then is distinctively Christian? And then he or she may be sent in quest of that in Christian life and in Christian story which is still miraculously there to be discovered and which can still both challenge and enrich the Platonist in all of us.

3   SYSTEMATIC THEOLOGY: INTERNECINE WARFARE

It would be wrong to read that last section as just another replay of the blame-the-Greeks game: true, the Greek religious experience was as powerful and attractive and at its best, we may believe, as divine in origin as any that human history has known; but it was no more impervious to radical enrichment by the distinctively Christian experience than was the Jewish experience out of which Christianity originally grew, and no less instructive to Christians in that which it saw most clearly. In any case, the game as it is usually played blames the Christian heretics for including too much of the Greek 'philosophical' spirit, and then suggests that it was largely through their influence that this spirit infected even the sounder, the orthodox parts of Christian theology. But one need only examine a little more closely the example with which we have just been dealing, the Christian 'dogma' of God as Trinity, to realize that this is indeed a very unbalanced account of that historic achievement.

The heretics in our example were the followers of one Arius who preached his version of the Christian 'dogma' of God as Trinity from the pulpit at Alexandria at the beginning of the fourth century AD. They, like their opponents, made full use of the Greek theology of distinguishable *hypostases* (in the West *'persons'*) in the one divine being, but they insisted that these distinctions amounted to *differences* in the being or substance of God (the Greek word *ousia* can be translated either 'being' or 'substance') and that these differences in turn amounted to the fact that the 'persons' in this Trinity were successively lower in the scale of being the closer, as it were, they approached to the world in the very process of the divine creative and salvific outreach. So the Word which took origin from the One was by that very fact a lower level divinity than the One who had no origin at all, and the same could be said, *a fortiori*, for the Spirit sent by the Word into the world. Put in another way, Word and Spirit were agents of the One in the creation and salvation of the world, and they were therefore more subject to change than was the One. The Arians never denied the divinity of the Word; that was a slander upon them which was enthusiastically propagated by their opponents, but they did insist that these divine 'persons' were all different in being, not 'one in being', and successively subordinate one to the other.

Now the logic of this position, given the common borrowing by both sides of 'pagan' Greek theological concepts, was quite strong, and so the opponents of the Arians, to whom history has ceded the palm of orthodoxy, were often driven by the point and power of this logic to positions which they might not otherwise have occupied. For in order to evade the Arian argument that divine 'persons' who were intimately engaged in the vagaries of history must be thought mutable and therefore different and lower than the utterly immutable One, the orthodox concentrated more and more upon the impervious status of Word and Spirit, and as a consequence they distanced Word and Spirit more and more from all that was done and suffered on earth. They were driven to speculate more and more about inner

divine processes 'before' or 'beyond' anything which they believed as disciples of Jesus that God had done in this world, and
simultaneously they arrived at a more immutable, impervious
divinity than any Greek had ever imagined.

To say this is not necessarily to commend the view of Emil
Brunner that the inner-divine Trinity of three utterly immutable 'persons', existing alongside of one another, distinct but
identical in all eternity, was an aberration of Christian theological thought, and that Christians can speak only of a Trinity
of divine 'persons' in the action, and in the order, of God's
outreach to the world. Nor is the intention here to reverse the
verdict of the historical Church as to who were·the winners and
who the losers on that ancient theological battleground. Undoubtedly the Christian faith could̄ not then and cannot now
tolerate the suggestion of divine beings different from, and
lower than, the God who was in Jesus reconciling the world to
himself. Nevertheless, one can clearly see, if only with the invidious wisdom of hindsight, that both heretics and orthodox
were in significant instances wide of the mark. Neither seemed
to realize, for example, that a faith which had at its centre a
crucified God could well regard the greater and greater involvement of God in the vicissitudes of this world and its history,
as signs of 'greater' rather than 'lesser' divinity, if one can use
such language. The Arians were sensitive to the suffering of
divinity in Jesus, but saw that as diminution of full divine status;
the orthodox were adamant in their refusal of lower divine
'persons', but could secure their position only by a retreat into
pre-existence and an image of identical divine 'persons' more
immutable than ever.

But the major part of this example in this secion is to illustrate,
however sketchily, the main effect upon the exercise of dogmatic
theology of internecine battles between Christians. The main
effect is to drive each side to extremes of formulation which in
more eirenic circumstances they would not have adopted and
simultaneously to blind both sides to a broader or deeper, in any
event, a truer conception of their common faith. Now this point
would not be such a serious one, nor need it take up so much
space in so short a chapter of so short a book, if the instances of
belligerent disagreement between Christians were relatively
rare. Unfortunately, however, they are far from rare. The Chris-

tian faith has been marred from the beginning, not by different interpretations in theory and in practice, for such could promise nothing less than continuous and mutual enrichment of the Christian experience of life, but by a persistent chauvinism, a particular pride, and an ensuing belligerence which, though tragically evident in all areas of Christian living, finds its most permanent form in the *odium theologicum*, the self-hatred of the theological community down the ages.

This is a factor which affects not merely the settled and commonly accepted 'dogmas' about God and Jesus which are the common Christian inheritance from the first five centuries, but also the more fluid doctrines of the Christian faith, many of which came into bitter contention at the time of the Protestant Reformation. So it might be well to take another example, one which leads more directly to our next topic: the issue between Romans and Reformers concerning Scripture and tradition.

The Protestant Reformers of the sixteenth century were quite right about the corruption of Christianity, and quite right, of course, also in blaming this upon the works of man rather than the grace of God. And since both sides in the ensuing debate considered the Scriptures to be entirely inspired and utterly infallible – indeed the Roman Catholic authorities maintained a much harder line on these attributes of Scripture long after most Protestant groups had at least nuanced the latter – the debate inevitably settled on the nature and the role of church tradition. The slogans which brought this debate to battle pitch are only too well known. The Protestants cried 'Scriptura sola: Scripture alone'; the Romans retorted that God's revelation through Jesus via his apostles had come down in Scripture and tradition (though the Council of Trent itself rather wisely refused to 'partition' the revelation in any way between these twin streams which carried it down to us). And as the heat of battle grew both sides found themselves driven to more and more extreme positions, and both sides lost sight of the true breadth and depth, indeed of the full Christian truth of the subjects which they then so manfully bowdlerized.

For both sides, inevitably perhaps, began to treat tradition as a kind of dead thing from the past – well, at least a finished product, and the only truly finished products are dead ones – a kind of deposit of dogmas and rites and conventions. The

Protestants set themselves to argue that some of these (the ones they did not find in Scripture) were corruptions. The Romans set about defending some of them (not all) in a variety of ways, but ultimately by appealing to the allegedly God-given authority vested in doctrinal matters in the Roman hierarchy – an argument which the Protestants not unnaturally considered somewhat circular, if not downright self-serving.

What both sides were actually doing in the course, and in the aftermath, of the Protestant Reformation was this: they were *both* creating out of their Christian past forms of Christian life and community which had never before existed in just that way. For as George Tavard once put it, 'Tradition exists only as a contemporary interpretation of the past in the light of the expected future';[2] and both sides were giving new contemporary interpretations of the past in theory and in act as they tried to shape the Christian future. Both sides were creating Christian tradition, for tradition exists only in the act of creaturely creation. But their mutual adoption of the fighting mode made both sides misunderstand what they were about, and the victim of the bitter fight was the most explicit subject of their theological attention: the concept of Christian tradition.

As a theological concept in Christianity, tradition can refer to nothing less than the Christian life coursing through history. This is most visible as the life of the Christian community in the world, which lives, its members believe, as the Body of Christ animated by the Spirit which is its risen Lord. Hence the paradigm for the understanding of Christian tradition is the Christian Eucharist, in which all Christian Churches confess, whatever the differences in their eucharistic *theologies*, that the risen Jesus is really present. Eucharist is the *anamnesis* of the death of Jesus, the act in which he touched eternal life. It is a rich and complex action in which people take bread 'which earth has given and human hands have made', bless God for it as a symbol of all life, break it as an earnest of breaking open one's closed and fearful existence, and give to others as a small symbolic extension of the amazing grace received. Simultaneously the story is told, mainly from Scripture, prayers rise up from the heart (for this is an astounding thing which is here attempted), efforts are made to understand and to expound. Faith is evoked, inspired, shaped and pointed for Christian action; and the tender shoots of invincible hope are nurtured.

Now *there* is tradition *in nuce.* And what a rich and complex thing it truly is; what a sequence of creative moments in which the past *lives* and the future is born. And yet, if one listened to the proud protagonists of Protestant and Roman theologies of tradition one would get the distinct impression that the Christian faith consisted primarily in sets of 'dogmas', largely if not exclusively verbal entities, which the Protestants hunted for in Scripture and the Romans in history and Scripture, so that salvation seemed to be secured by saying the right thing (confessing, if you prefer) – while believing it to be true, of course.

It is within the rich and complex eucharistic life of the Christian community in the world that the 'monuments' of tradition find their relevance: the ancient rituals and institutions, the prayers and hymns, the commentaries on Scripture, even the theologies, of faithful Christians of old. It is there too that Scripture itself is read, its inspiring Spirit answering to the Spirit that still enlivens the Body of Christ. It is therefore within this same eucharistic life of the Christian community in the world that the question of relative authorities, of supreme and secondary norms, and so on, can find its only acceptable solutions, provided that all authority is understood in its radical Christian revision, as a service to life and not lording it over anyone.

Those who engaged in battle about the concept of tradition misunderstood, all of them, the essential reference of that concept to Christian life coursing through the world. And as a direct consequence of the impression they conveyed that Christianity consists primarily in 'dogmas' (in Scripture or out of Scripture) they damaged the very normative nature of Scripture which all of them with their lips professed. But that is a point for the next section. For the purpose of ending this section it is necessary only to note this further example of the way in which belligerent polemics drive both sides to extreme positions and blind both sides to the real riches of Christian truth. In this particular case their mutually inflicted misunderstanding expressed itself, with fine irony, in their inability to sit together at the Lord's table.

4 DOGMA AND SCRIPTURE

One of the principal points of the last section was to demonstrate the deleterious effects of polemics upon any subject which is made an object of its invidious attention. Both sides in the post-Reformation era equally, if in their different ways, misunderstood the Christian tradition. But the damage, great as it was, could not be contained at that level; and that is the point that must now be developed. The Christian Scriptures are so intimately involved in Christian tradition that every misunderstanding of the latter is bound to affect in an adverse fashion the normative role of Scripture, no matter how often or how pompously that is proclaimed. This is true, whether we are thinking of their origins, their ecclesiastical recognition and preservation, or indeed of the reading and exposition of their contents which has been absolutely central to Christians' understanding of their faith from the beginning – Aquinas' commentaries on Scripture make up the largest bulk of his writings and provide the inspiration of their whole corpus.

The matter here is further complicated, *and* further damaged, by the fact that Romans and Protestants make this very issue of the normative nature of Scripture a further bone of contention between them. Protestants maintain that the Roman Pope's claim to supreme doctrinal authority and in particular to infallibility in his most solemn pronouncements on matters of faith and morals, clearly implies that he considers his teaching more normative than the Scriptures'. The Pope entirely rejects this implication, claiming that he is totally under the authority of the Word of God which is contained in Scripture, and that the aid of the Spirit which is accorded to the whole Church and to him and to his hierarchy as its officers, is designed to keep them faithful to this Word in the exercise of doctrinal authority and never in any way to supersede it. Furthermore, the Romans are often anxious to add, if one waits for a little while after the Protestant has proclaimed the Scriptures as the supreme norm of his Christian faith, one will find that the formulae he uses to present this faith derive directly from one of his favourite Confessions (the *Westminster Confession,* for example) or repeat some doctrinal slogan of a great Reformer. About such formulae he proves quite as intransigent as any Pope. He maintains, of course, that he is intransigent about such formulae only because they do faithfully represent the truth of Scripture – and then he goes off to assemble his particular selection of proof-texts. And so does the Pope!

Much the same point can be illustrated from those commonly received doctrinal formulae which were hammered out by great councils of the early Church such as Nicaea and Chalcedon. Try the simple experiment of saying something critical – just critical, mind you, not dismissive – about the two-nature Christology of Chalcedon or about the fourth-century doctrine of the Trinity which finally derived from the Nicene definition. No matter how much you protest that your criticism is based upon richer and deeper sources in Scripture, you will arouse the instant ire of Romans and Protestants alike, both equally unwilling to concede that any doctrinal formula for understanding Jesus and God could be scriptural if it attempts in any way to modify, much less to replace these. It is in the course of such experiences that one may beg leave to doubt the truth – though perhaps not the sincerity – of the contention on both sides that the Scriptures are the supreme norm of the faith. Indeed, we have already suggested, these early doctrinal formulae, which are now so commonly received, were themselves in their time the formulae by which one Christian party sought victory over another Christian party. So in all kinds of formulae, both those which unite us today and those which divide us, we must be prepared to look for norms to which Scripture is then forced to comply, and we must always, unfortunately, be suspicious of stout declarations that Scripture is the supreme norm of the faith.

It should now be possible to put the kind of flesh which the systematic theologian would like to see on the skeletal structure which the analysis in the first chapter so well discerned by use of the category of 'horizons'; mental and cultural horizons from which the modern person approaches the faith, and the very different horizon which was that of the first writers and readers of the New Testament. General advice to the effect that the horizons are different, and that readers of the New Testament must be aware of this, is welcome. Specific examples of the altered meanings of terms still in use are essential. But there are two movements which, following upon the analysis of this chapter so far, the systematician would want to recommend, before any hope could be held out that the fruitful merging of these horizons could take place, in which presuppositions become conscious and are put in question, and new understanding results.

First, it is necessary for each Christian inquirer to endeavour to understand with empathy the positions adopted by separated Christian brethren. The motive here is not the modern ecumenical one, though that motive is admirable in its own right. The motive now is no less than the rediscovery of the Christian truth through the initial acknowledgement that all polemics always distort one's own version of the truth, if in no other way than by narrowing it to the exclusion of that part of a fuller version of the truth which one's hostility prevents one from seeing in the formulations of the other party. It is necessary to stress that this initial move is absolutely unavoidable if there is to be any hope of recovering once more in the modern age the rich theologies contained in Scripture in all the variety of their literary forms. For there is not a single area of Christian doctrine which has not at some time in the course of the Christian tradition been narrowed or distorted by the cut and thrust of polemics; and therefore all of our inherited presuppositions about the Christian faith need to become reflectively conscious of the manner in which polemics have made them what they are. The only way in which this can take place is by re-enacting the battle, but now as a friendly game in which one is prepared to change sides and to experience the other's position in both defence and attack. The very least of the gains scored in such an amicable replay will be a recovery of Christian charity, which is, after all, more important than any doctrine. Nor need this necessary exercise be hindered by fears that all distinction between heresy and orthodoxy will disappear and loyalty to the truth will be replaced by a bland indifference. On the contrary, error is more easily detectable when one is prepared to acknowledge that those one would otherwise wish to describe simply as enemies were not altogether unsuccessful in a genuine wish to reach the truth; and when one is consequently prepared to admit that error is as likely on one's own side as it is on the other. In any case, the facts are indisputable. All areas of Christian doctrine have been narrowed and distorted by perennial Christian polemics. There is now no way for any Christian to escape the limits of the presuppositions which this fact implies, than by engaging in a sympathetic study of hitherto rival versions of Christian truth and life. The effect of this kind of narrowness and distortion will be removed only when its cause is acknowledged and the influence of that cause reversed. In practice this means that no faculty of Christian theology should now exist which does not have an active input from representatives of different Christian traditions. It remains, however, right and good that different Christian traditions should continue to enrich the Church universal and that faculties with traditional allegiances should therefore continue to exist.

Second, something very similar must be said about the broader cultures within which Christians have up to now conducted their seemingly interminable arguments. Here also, before any hopes of success can be entertained for the difficult project of seeing simultaneously the horizon of the scriptural authors and the horizon of their modern readers, the latter must make a very deliberate effort indeed to assimilate with great empathy the dominant 'philosophical' movements of their contemporary culture. For, like the Christians of the first five centuries, modern readers of the Bible are heavily influenced by dominant cultural trends. They are all the more heavily influenced the more oblivious of such trends they are or are determined to be, and the more unconsciously in consequence the influence operates. Furthermore, the word 'philosophical' is placed in inverted commas because, despite some appearances to the contrary, there is as much reason now as there was in the age of Platonism to see in these alternatives rivals to Christianity at a truly religious depth. Admittedly late Western culture has seen a growth of atheism as a genuine cultural option for masses of people, an option which Western culture did not see before, if indeed any culture did. Nevertheless it is a mistake to regard Marxism, for instance, or some still influential forms of existentialism, as atheistic first and foremost. Like the more diffuse forms of humanism in modern times, these major movements, as their most prominent spokespersons have untiringly pointed out, are first and foremost humanistic. They involve the death of the dominant (Christian) God – other gods are scarcely affected by their critique – only because that God, as his followers have portrayed him, is quite palpably irrelevant to the projects

of creative human freedom, and is in many respects a positive
hindrance to these on both the social and the individual levels.
Hence Feuerbach, the great nineteenth-century popularizer of
this kind of humanism, said: 'What today is called atheism,
tomorrow will be called religion.' For as this popular foster-
father of modern humanism insisted, the plan was to bring
down to earth goals worthy of human existence, values which
people had mistakenly worshipped as an alien god in an empty
heaven. And it really is the case that contemporary Western
humanism has consistently sought systems of value which
would rival in height and depth and comprehensiveness the old
(Christian) religious absolutes. Any modern humanist, Marxist
or otherwise, who is tempted to deny this can be asked one
simple question: Do you or do you not endorse warfare? An
affirmative answer to that question, whatever the conditions
with which it is hedged, implies absolutes. For anyone who asks
me to offer my life, particularly in the effort to take someone
else's life, is asking me to deal in absolutes – I have nothing,
literally nothing, greater to give than life, and I cannot reasonably be asked to give it for anything less than a life that is
deathless. Dealing in death, as all dealing in war is dealing in
death, is dealing in absolutes, and all known forms of modern
humanism deal in war. That logic at least is irrefragible, no
matter how many people try to evade its inevitable conclusion.

The modern 'atheistic' rivals to Christianity, then, do move
at the same depth and with the same comprehensiveness as the
old religious visions which they have sought with much recent
success to replace. Even before the other world religions make
their increasing influence felt in a shrinking world, therefore,
Christians are already breathing in the cultural air of humanist
systems which are as 'religious', that is to say, as deeply and
comprehensively 'binding', as their own faith. This fact will
have some repercussions on our thoughts about the nature of
faith in the concluding section of this chapter. For the moment
it is necessary to note only that, as in the case of our predecessors, there is no short cut to an awareness of the extent of the
influence of these dominant cultural movements on what we
might be tempted to consider pure formulations of the Christian
faith. Indeed just as some or our earliest predecessors issued
rounded embargoes against all 'pagan philosophy', and prob-

ably felt that that was good protection against their influence, so today we find high officers of the Roman Church issuing similar embargoes on Marxism. But, apart altogether from the fact that Marx promoted values which many Christians still significantly neglect and from which they still have a very great deal to learn, Marxism has long entered the blood-streams of contemporary humanity and such embargoes are about as effective as a vow of temperance taken just as a policeman is about to administer a breathalizer.

It is only when one has studied with every sympathy the theologies of one's separated Christian brethren that one can realize how far one's own theology has been driven and narrowed by polemical extent; and it is only when one has studied with every sympathy those religious or quasi-religious movements which achieve some level of dominance in one's culture that one can realize how much one has unconsciously absorbed and then passed off as Christian. In both cases the realization will require adjustment, but in neither case need it require the cruel choice of either losing one's identity or rejecting all that one can attribute to the other, the good as well as the bad. On the contrary, empathy can reveal the bad and the narrow in one's own tradition; it can see the good in the other as well as the bad; and it can simultaneously show how one can enhance the distinctive form in which one can recover the best in one's own tradition, assimilate some of the good from the others, and rejoice in the richness of those distinctive forms which other traditions possess but which one does not share.

All Christian systematic theology from the beginning has been formed in the hot flames of polemics and in the forges of contemporary cultures. In consequence these two specific studies, viz., the study of other Christian traditions and the study of dominant cultural movements, are equally and alike necessary for anyone who would try today to understand the biblical documents in their time from the perspectives which are so insidiously influential in ours. Both studies, in their different but complementary ways, make us aware of the limits of our modern minds and, with the skilful aid of the exegete, enable us to discover the different minds of New Testament peoples and to be questioned in our turn by the documents they bequeathed to us.

5   SYSTEMATIC THEOLOGY AND FAITH

The main question which concerns the writers and, we hope, the readers of this book, viz., the relationship between Bible and systematic or dogmatic theology, is often in these days turned into the question of the relationship between history and faith. Some of the many forms of this questionable transformation have already been pointed up in the course of the first chapter, when presenting the views, for example, that the findings of New Testament study were descriptive rather than prescriptive, or 'merely', or 'strictly' historical. Now the main sources of the introduction into the matter which here concerns us of questionable distinctions between history and faith have undoubtedly been the systematicians and some noted biblical scholars behaving as systematicians.

'Theology is a function of the Church',[3] wrote Karl Barth at the opening of his monumental *Church Dogmatics*, and shortly afterwards he is explaining to his readers why dogmatics demands faith. In this at least there is no difference between Barth and Schleiermacher. Those who take the trouble to read Schleiermacher himself rather than the common caricatures of his work produced particularly by Barthians, will notice that he too, at the beginning of *The Christian Faith*, disclaims any intention of establishing Christian doctrine 'on a foundation of general principles'. On the contrary, since dogmatics can only be done in the Church, he begins his first chapter with a definition of the Christian Church and ends by insisting that 'there is no other way of obtaining participation in the Christian communities than through faith in Jesus as Redeemer'.[4] Hence the broadest possible spectrum of theological opinion is agreed in requiring faith for dogmatics. But it was a great biblical scholar, acting as systematician, who drew the clearest distinction between this faith and the 'history' that is involved in the scientific study of the scriptural sources. Rudolf Bultmann was not the first to draw the distinction between history and faith, nor was he even the first to drive that distinction into the very centre of the being of Christ, where it became the distinction between the Jesus of history and the Christ of faith. He was however, the one whose great scholarly stature so popularized that distinction in this century that very many Christians still feel today that they must choose between history and faith, that history is the obvious option for a self-styled scientific age, and that some sort of special plea must be made if considerations concerning religious faith are also to be admitted.

Now when one sees such separation of faith from history (and from 'science' or 'reason', to which history belongs) agreed by 'believers' and 'unbelievers' alike, one may very well suspect that one is in the presence of a deep and broad cultural prejudice, a prejudice so deep and so broad that it is quite unlikely to have been brought about by a group of systematicians and exegetes, however individually influential they may have been. And indeed this prejudice does coincide with the rise of alternative, atheistic 'philosophies' in the Western culture, and it takes the form of a mistaken belief that these are as different from the Christianity they sought to replace as something called 'reason' is from something called 'faith'. In actual fact it was the bitter polemics between the old Christians and the new humanists which bred and nurtured the mistaken belief that faith and reason were contraries. A wiser theory of knowledge would realize that all human convictions are forms of more or less rational belief. The truth of the matter is that all human beings live by faith all of the time, faith in science, faith in leaders, faith in national power, faith in money, reasonable faith, irrational faith, and quite frequently faith which is truly pathetic; and as the last section asserted, the substitute absolutes are plentifully present in the new humanisms, however loudly they proclaim their independence of the old religion. History the reality – and, if it ever proves adequate to its fuller task, history the science – will eventually show to this erratic race which of all the rival absolutes is the most benign.

When it is said, then, that systematic theology can be properly pursued only by those who have faith or are at least capable of faith, it cannot be the intention to point to a predetermined number of people – all baptized Christians, for example – as the ones who are alone capable of this exercise. For, however much Christians may say that faith is a gift of God (isn't everything?), they cannot mean either that their faith is then a secure possession, or that it is totally different in kind from all other forms of deep and comprehensive faith which are, like it, a human phenomenon. On the contrary, Christian faith is a constant mixture of fidelity and infidelity in answer to a call, an invitation which Christians believe comes from God through Jesus. And that human answer is similar in kind to other erratic human answers to the call of other absolutes. To say that systematic theology can only be exercised by those who have faith is to say that a particular faith can only be properly expounded by those who attempt to live by it; but this assertion recognizes that it is true also of other faiths, even atheistic faiths so-called. Nor does it rule out the possibility of a follower of one faith genuinely studying another. A recognition of the faith by which one lives, together with an essential exercise of empathy, will enable any human being to study the systematic theology of another faith.

If that were not the case, any substantial difference in the faith experience of human beings would prevent their systematic explanation to each other. And what account should we then give of the spread of Christianity – an explanation cast wholly in terms of divine interventionism, in consequence of which the new converts could talk only to themselves? And how, in the final analysis, should we account for the Christian claim that latter-day Christians who have gone astray in their Christian faith can have the error of their ways corrected by that normative exposition of the faith of their earliest predecessors which we call the New Testament?

For – and this is the second conclusion to this final section – to say that the documents of the New Testament are faith documents, artistic and theological expositions of the faith of the first Christians, is to place them within rather than outside things human. And the fact that the formal study of these early expositions of the faith is called 'history' is due solely to their belonging to the past. The study of contemporary expositions of a similar or different faith could be called something else, but the difficulties and the promises of success would be the same in both cases, except that the wider context and some of the particular details of contemporary or near-contemporary expositions would obviously be more easily available. But we should in both cases be attempting to proceed from faith to faith, from the faith by which we live to the faith by which others live or have lived, so that we should become more conscious, at one and the same time, of our faith and of theirs, and then attempt the difficult but necessary task of discerning the spirits within these faiths, looking as we do so for the guidance of the God or the Absolute we believe is beckoning to us.

Faith is the skin in which we, all of us, dance our lives away. There are different faiths, as there are people with different coloured skins; but there are no skinless people, only skinless sausages. The historian is always a man or woman of some faith and if he or she touches the human at any point of investigation into the past, contact with the faith of others is absolutely unavoidable, the beliefs by which people lived and for which all too frequently, as history shows, they died. History is a field-encompassing field, someone said, and undoubtedly some of the fields encompassed within this complicated discipline are 'scientific' in a very stringent sense of that word: dating objects or documents, classifying, translating. But history in its encompassing sense does work from faith to faith, and these 'scientific' operations are merely contributory to its larger task. History in itself in fact embodies and illustrates most of the problems which these two chapters have analysed, most of them variations of the problem of the merging of the different horizons of different human faiths. There is therefore nothing in the least incongruous about history studying faith-documents such as those that make up the New Testament, even if in these examples the faith in question is more explicitly the subject of the authors than is the case with most documents with which historians deal.

And so, having set in perspective the general problems of the New Testament foundations of Christian theology, it is time to take up some concrete examples.

NOTES

1 Karl Marx, *The Poverty of Philosophy* (Peking 1978), p. 115.
2 Joseph E. Kelly, ed., *Perspectives on Scripture and Tradition* (Notre Dame, Fides, 1976), p. 92.
3 Karl Barth, *Church Dogmatics* (Edinburgh, T. & T. Clark, 1975), vol. I, Part I, p. 3.
4 F. Schleiermacher, *The Christian Faith* (Edinburgh, T. & T. Clark, 1976), p. 68.

3

First Test Case – Christology
(1) A View from New Testament Theology

The most obvious and pressing test case for the dialogue which is NT theology is provided by Christology. For Jesus clearly stands at the centre of faith and thought for the NT writers as a whole. And it is the faith focused on Jesus which more or less from the beginning has provided the principal reason and inspiration for Christianity's distinctiveness. Here if anywhere the importance and character of the dialogue will become clear.

We shall consider three passages which have had incalculable influence in the subsequent self-understanding and formulation of Christian belief regarding Jesus: Colossians 1.15–20, the birth narratives of Matthew and Luke, and the Johannine claim for Christ summed up in John 14.6.

1 COLOSSIANS 1.15–20

15 He is the image of the invisible God, the firstborn of all creation;
16 For in him were created all things in heaven and on earth
...
all things were created through him and to him.
17 He is before all things,
and in him all things hold together
18 And he is the head of the body (the church).

He is the beginning, the firstborn from the dead,
in order that in all things he might be pre-eminent.
19 For in him God in all his fulness was pleased to dwell,
20 And through him to reconcile all things to him,
making peace (through the blood of his cross) through him,
Whether things on earth or things in heaven.

In terms of Christology the sense and significance of the passage seems to be straightforward: the passage is a clear statement of the deity and pre-existence of Christ. And so it has been classically understood. From the perspective of Christian tradition we have one of the earliest and clearest expressions of the role of the second person of the Trinity in creation and salvation. With appropriate elaboration this interpretation would provide the opening statement from one side of the dialogue.

From the other side the dialogue can begin most simply by posing the question: Would this interpretation express the meaning intended by the original author? The answer would have to be No! (however qualified) – at least in the sense that the Christian who formulated this text and the Christians who first received it had not yet conceived of the Trinity or defined such distinctions within the one God of Christian faith. The interpretation of Col. 1.15–20 in terms of the Trinity is the fruit of debate and reflection *subsequent* to the first definitive formulation of the text.

To make this initial judgement does not mean that we dispense with or discard the classic Christian interpretation, for that remains one element or partner in the continuing dialogue. Moreover, there are still crucial questions to be resolved: Is the classic interpretation simply a restatement in terms of the later debates of what was there in the text anyway, expressed in different terms? What was it in or about the text which made it possible so to interpret it? Nor does this judgement pre-empt the question of whether the original meaning is or should be finally authoritative for the Christian. How proper was it for the Fathers of the Church so to interpret the text? All these point to further aspects or stages of the dialogue to which we must return. But for the moment in pursuing the exegetical task it is necessary to go *behind* the classic understanding of the text. It is necessary, since otherwise the dialogue cannot even begin properly, necessary if we are to allow the original intention of the Christian author of the passage to have a role in the dialogue as independent of our own perspective as possible.

In taking up this exegetical challenge it is fortunately not necessary to pursue several important exegetical issues – including the question of original authorship (a pre-Pauline but

Christian hymn? – most would say Yes), the question of authorship of the letter (most would say Paul), and the question of
whether and if so how much Paul has changed the hymn in
taking it over (not much – the most likely additions are indicated
by brackets). In a full-scale dialogue these questions would have
to be dealt with since they obviously affect the particular context
of the passage, and the different possible answers would inevitably refine the exegesis in a number of ways. But for the
purposes of this example we can restrict ourselves to the major
christological issue, which is largely unaffected by these other
questions.

When we try to set the Christology of the Colossians passage
into its *broader* historical context the key factor becomes the
influence of *Wisdom* language and ideas. Within the ancient
Near East, reflection on and pursuit of wisdom, human and
divine, was a major preoccupation. The principal stream within
early Judaism flows through Proverbs, ben Sira (Ecclesiasticus),
the Wisdom of Solomon and the Jewish Alexandrian philosopher Philo, and represents an important aspect of Judaism's
own dialogue and interaction with the surrounding cultures,
religions and philosophies. Influence from this Jewish wisdom
tradition on Col. 1.15–20 has been recognized from earliest days
in Christian use of the passage, but its extent has been documented more fully in recent years and can be illustrated quite
easily, particularly with regard to the first three verses.

Col. 1.15 – the image of God.	Wisd. 7.26 – Wisdom 'an image of God's goodness' Philo, *Leg. All.* 1.43 – Wisdom the 'image' and 'vision of God'
Col. 1.15 – the firstborn of all creation.	Prov. 8.22, 25 – Wisdom as the first creation Philo, *Qu. Gen.* 4.97 – 'the firstborn mother of all things'
Col. 1.16a – in him were created all things.	Ps. 104.24 – 'in/by wisdom he made all things' Wisd. 8.5 – Wisdom 'who effects all things'
Col. 1.16c – all things were created through him.	Prov. 3.19 – 'The Lord by wisdom founded the earth' Philo, *Det.* 54 – 'Wisdom through

	whom the universe was completed'
Col. 1.17a – he is before all things.	Prov. 8.26–7 – 'Before he made the earth...I was there'
	Ecclus. 1.4; 24.9 – 'created before all things' 'in the beginning'
Col. 1.17b – in him all things hold together	Ecclus. 43.26 'By his word all things hold together'

These parallels make it sufficiently clear that the Colossian hymn is drawing on a prominent strand within Jewish reflection about creation. Christ is being spoken of in terms which anyone familiar with the Jewish wisdom tradition would recognize. What the Jewish writers said about divine wisdom, the Colossian hymn says about Jesus. But what is the significance of this fact? Would it be fair to say, for example, that Jesus was being identified with divine Wisdom? Or indeed that divine Wisdom had become incarnate in Jesus?

Much depends on how divine Wisdom should be understood. Three main options have been canvassed in the exegetical debate of the past few years.

(a) Wisdom is a *divine being*, an independent deity, distinct from God. This is how Wisdom could and usually was understood within the wider polytheism of the nations and religions surrounding ancient Israel. The possibility cannot be entirely ruled out that the Jewish wisdom tradition in adopting such language into its own theologizing also imported an element of syncretistic polytheism. If so, then Judaism (or at least the Hellenistic Judaism represented in the wisdom tradition) had already began to qualify the fundamental Jewish creed that God is one. And if that is so, then the Christianity which used such language of Jesus was simply elaborating this Jewish redefinition of God: Jesus was the second God in heaven, the High God's 'junior partner'. In other words, if option (a) gives us the right historical context within which to understand Col. 1.15–20, we may find ourselves forced to the uncomfortable conclusion that this very early expression of Christology was basically polytheistic (two gods) in orientation. In which case the subsequent interpretation of the passage would rank as an attempt to reclaim it for orthodoxy.

(b) The second option currently much favoured is that in Jewish usage divine wisdom was simply a *personification*. However the female figure of Wisdom was conceptualized in the surrounding cultures, within Judaism itself Wisdom was never thought of as a divine being distinct from God, as God's female consort. She was simply a way of speaking about God himself, about God in his self-revelation and activity towards and within his creation, about the feminine in God. This would certainly make better sense of various features of Jewish thought in this area. (1) Divine wisdom is always thought of as God's wisdom, that is, God acting wisely towards his own (e.g. Prov. 2.6; Ecclus. 1.1; Wisd. 8.21—9.2; Philo, *Leg. All.* 3.99; *Sac.* 64). Hence, what is attributed to Wisdom is also attributed to God (e.g. Wisd. 10—11), and attributed to God without remainder (e.g. Ecclus. 18. 1–4), because wisdom *is* God. (2) The wisdom imagery is simply an extended example of the vigour and vividness of Jewish poetic speech in which other manifestations of the divine ordering of history could be personified – such as 'faithfulness' or God's 'hand' or 'arm' (e.g. Ps. 85. 10–11; Isa. 51.9). In other words, the 'wisdom of God', like other near synonyms ('word of God', 'spirit of God', 'glory of God', etc.), functions as a way of speaking of the immanence of God in and to his world. By means of such vivid personifications the involvement of God with humankind can be expressed without detracting from his transcendence.

(c) The third option recognizes the strength of both the previous options and the degree to which they seem to cancel each other out, and so looks for a middle way. Wisdom is neither a separate being from God, nor simply a way of speaking about God, but a *hypostasis*, a something in between separate personality and abstract entity. In speaking of Jesus in these terms, the Colossian hymn presents Jesus as such a divine hypostasis. Such a view is obviously attractive for our understanding of how the distinctive Christian view of the Trinity emerged – not least since it uses the distinctive term ('hypostasis') which provided the key description for the crucial distinction within the Godhead (one essence, three hypostases). If indeed the Jewish understanding of the relation between God and divine wisdom can fairly be conceptualized by means of this word, then the subtle Christian definition of the Godhead, or at least of the place of Christ within the Godhead, can be said to have been anticipated by the Jewish wisdom tradition. In which case Col. 1.15–20 is merely a transition from a form of Jewish Binitarianism to the full-blown Christian Trinitarianism.

The trouble with this last option, however, is that it makes use of a technical term ('hypostasis') which gained this distinctive meaning only as a result of the later Christian controversies. It was precisely as a way of resolving the problem of distinguishing between the persons of the Godhead that the word 'hypostasis' was given this fine gradation of meaning. That is to say, the conceptuality which distinguishes between (a) and (b) was not yet current at the time of the Jewish wisdom writers, or of Paul. Had it indeed been already current, and already quite acceptable by virtue of its use in the wisdom tradition, the application of such categories to Jesus would have been unlikely to create such opposition from the Jewish side. But in fact, in Jewish eyes, the subsequent Christian attempts to define the place of Christ within the Godhead came to be regarded as an abandonment of the unity of God, and as such a fundamental heresy.

The same point can be made against the first option (a). For had Jewish theology in its wisdom strand found itself able to incorporate the much more widespread forms of polytheism within its system, they would have been less likely to reject Christianity's claims regarding Christ. In other words, the more firmly we recognize monotheism to be a fundamental part of Jewish theology, the more we are pushed towards the second option (b) – divine wisdom as a way of speaking about God in his availability and nearness to his creatures.

All this, however, only fills in something of the broad background of the Colossian hymn. Even if option (b) comes nearest of the three options to catching the Jewish understanding of Wisdom at the time of Paul, what does that enable us to say about the Colossian hymn itself? We can hardly dismiss the possibility that the hymn itself marks a stage beyond the previous Jewish wisdom thought. In fact the language of the hymn forces the same three options upon us.

(a) Does the hymn speak of Christ? Clearly so. But does it mean to ascribe that role in creation to *Jesus*, the man who ministered in Galilee and died on a cross in Jerusalem? That would be an obvious way to understand the hymn. But to say that the man Jesus was with God in the beginning and was God's agent in creation is not classic Christian doctrine. In classic Christology Jesus is the man that Wisdom *became* in the incarnation. Moreover, to ascribe the role of Wisdom in creation to the man Jesus Christ would seem to cross the boundary between monotheism and polytheism. For the second person of the Trinity would then be a 'person' in the modern sense, a person as Jesus was a person. And if God consists of three such persons then God is three and not one. It is no surprise that some sects like the Mormons have followed the logic of such interpretation and understand the Trinity as indeed three immortal beings.

Here again, of course, we must beware lest the different partners in the dialogue become confused and must continue to insist that the Colossian hymn be read first in terms of the categories and conceptualities of its own day without letting the logic and concerns of the later debates determine its meaning for us. But even so it remains unlikely that a firmly monotheistic Jew like Paul would have compromised his monotheism to such an extent as to attribute primeval deity to Jesus as such, the junior member of an original two God team. Even less likely that a Christianity which espoused such an abandonment of Jewish monotheism continued to remain as acceptable in Jewish circles as Christianity did for some decades to come. And still more unlikely that subsequent Christology was able to pull back from such a developed polytheistic position to retrieve its monotheistic claims in the subsequent debates.

(c) Could it be the case that the Colossian hymn itself has moved the thought and conceptuality available to it beyond whatever point it had already reached? Even if the sort of distinction represented by the word 'hypostasis' in its later meaning was not yet conceived prior to Paul, could it be that the very application of wisdom language to Christ was sufficient in itself to move the thought and conceptuality into that range of meaning? The suggestion is certainly attractive, but there are several indications in the hymn itself that this was not yet the case.

(1) A crucial phrase in the whole discussion is the one at the end of the first line – 'the firstborn of all creation'. In the light of the parallels with Wisdom cited above, the phrase is most probably intended to describe Christ as the first *creation* of God. As the parallels show, it was typical of the fluidity of Jewish talk (and thought) of Wisdom to describe her both as God's creation and as God's agent in creation. But this means that both the Jewish wisdom writers and Paul had not even begun to conceive of the kind of issues raised by later controversies – by Arius in particular who could cite this very text in favour of his belief that the Logos was a created being. In other words, the subtle shading of meaning which the later redefinition of 'hypostasis' provided (in response to Arius) is not present in the Colossian hymn. The hymnwriter seems to be moving still within the ambiguities and vaguer idioms of the Jewish wisdom tradition. The vivid metaphors and pictures of personification language do not lend themselves to such fine distinctions.

(2) In all this discussion the language of the second strophe (Col. 1.18b–20) is given far too little consideration. Here a striking fact is the way in which Christ's pre-eminence is spoken of as being a consequence of his resurrection (v.18b '…firstborn from the dead, that in everything he might be pre-eminent'). Even more striking is v.19. The precise force of 'all the fulness' is not clear, but the best way of translating the verse is probably as follows: 'in him God in all his fulness was pleased to dwell'. Both verses seem to give voice to a Christology of a significantly different order from that of the preceding wisdom Christology. For in this case the deity of Christ is not something attributed to him as from creation, but seems rather to be the result of 'God in all his fulness' choosing to dwell in the man Jesus (so that his death becomes an effective means of reconciliation – v.20). And his pre-eminence 'in all things' stems not from his involvement in creation but rather from his being 'the firstborn from the dead' in resurrection. Here again the thought is far removed from the later insistence that Christ was divine by nature, rather than by God's indwelling or by virtue of his resurrection. Not least of the awkwardness of this passage is that while the first verse seems to lend itself to an Arian view of

Christ, the second seems to lend itself to what would later be called an 'adoptionist' view of Christ (divine by adoption not by nature).

In short, when we pay attention to such uncomfortable exegetical features as those just itemized, (1) and (2), it becomes increasingly difficult to conclude that the Colossian hymnwriter (and Paul) had in mind the sort of distinctions which became fundamental in subsequent christological debate, and even more difficult to conclude that he (they) intended to exclude the possibility of understanding the hymn in an Arian-like or adoptionist-type way.

(b) The remaining alternative is (b) – that the language of the hymn was intended to identify Christ with the personification of God's outreach to his creation in revelation and redemption. God's wisdom is Christ – Christ as the definitive expression of God's active concern in creation and salvation. Such an understanding seems to make best sense of the Jewish background of a divine wisdom so vividly personified as to appear to be a divine being in her own right, separate from God. It fits well with the context of the middle of the first century, where the hymn does not seem to have been seen as a threat to or abandonment of Jewish monotheism. And, not least, it fits best with the content of the hymn as a whole, where the different emphases of the two strophes seem to pose the alternatives: either a 'straightforward' understanding of the language, leaving us with two contradictory tendencies (pre-existent deity and 'adoptionism'), or a recognition that the language is metaphorical and poetic and not to be taken literally. In short, a historically contextualized exegesis seems to point firmly to the conclusion that the hymnwriter did not intend to provide the careful definitions of analytical Christology, but was simply taking over for his own purposes the familiar poetic and personification imagery of the Jewish wisdom tradition.

We may see here a parallel also within Judaism – the fact that already for more than two centuries divine wisdom had been identified with the law (Ecclus. 24.23; Baruch 4.1). This too was in no way thought of as ascribing deity to the Torah. And the language of 'hypostasis' would be wholly inappropriate here. Rather, we have to recognize that such an identification was simply a way of pointing up the divine significance of the law – the Torah as the embodiment of God's revelation from the beginning. So, we may fairly judge, with the same identification of Christ as Wisdom. The vividness of the imagery used should not mislead, either into a form of polytheism or into a confused contradiction between pre-existent deity and adoptionism. It is simply the vigorously Jewish way of pointing up the divine significance of Christ. In contrast to the Jewish claims for the Torah, it is *Christ* who should be recognized as the embodiment of the divine wisdom from the beginning.

To sum up. Within its original context and in its original meaning, Col. 1.15–20 is probably best understood as an expression of Jewish monotheism. Believers in Christ, who were also familiar with the Jewish wisdom tradition, recognized the appropriateness of the wisdom imagery to describe the full significance of Christ. All that had been expressed by the wisdom imagery regarding God's action in creation, revelation and redemption could now be said of Christ, for in him that same power had come to its fullest and most definitive expression. That is to say, since Wisdom was not a divine being separate from God, but God himself in his self-revelation, so the wisdom Christology of the Colossian hymn is an expression of monotheistic faith. In other words, such an exegesis can not be regarded as diminishing the significance which the hymn ascribes to Christ. On the contrary, it brings out its full significance. For in the hymn Christ is presented not as the incarnation of a divine being somehow other than God, but of God himself. Christ is God's wisdom, God insofar as he can be known to his creatures, God insofar as he can make himself known to humankind.

If all this is so, then we have attained a clearer understanding of this important passage in its original and originally intended meaning. That meaning is not the same as the classical Christian interpretation of the passage. But that is not surprising, since the classical interpretation was formulated in the light of the subsequent debates which spanned the second to the fourth centuries. The point is that this recognition of the original scope of the passage's Christology makes it possible for theological use of the passage to proceed as a real dialogue, a real dialogue between historical text and authorial intention on the one hand

and subsequent concerns and issues on the other. And, more important, by thus clarifying the scope of the original text we have a yardstick (a canon) against which we can measure the validity of subsequent interpretations.

In this case the dialogue enables us to assess the crucial debates between Arius and Athanasius. Given the language of the passage both could cite it in their favour. But Arius in pressing the wisdom imagery of the text too literally lost hold of the essential function of wisdom Christology as an expression of monotheism. Whereas Athanasius and his successors by developing the idea of hypostasis were able to eliminate both the idea of Jesus as a second god and the idea of Christ's deity as something which God gave him in life or resurrection. That is to say, in the light of its original meaning we can say that the classic interpretation caught the central thrust of the hymn because it understood the hymn to speak of Jesus as the incarnation of the Logos, that is of God in his being for humankind.

A more controversial line of argument would be as follows. Col. 1.15–20 represents a monotheistic Christology within the less developed categories of the first century. Where issues had not yet crystallized, the broader and vaguer categories of wisdom imagery were fully appropriate. But subsequently, when specific issues had crystallized in the Arian controversy, definitions had to be found which did not give scope for such breadth and vagueness. From this two deductions might follow. (1) In christological controversy today, when issues are as vague and as undefined as they were in the first century (as is often the case outside academic circles), a broader formulation may still be quite acceptable. Within which, of course, the classic interpretation itself still forms the central option which can be restated when the issue narrows again in similar or equivalent terms to the classic christological debates (as still happens). (2) The interpretation of the classic credal patristic formulations must itself be measured by the canon of the original meaning of the Colossian hymn. Only so will they be retained in *their* central thrust as an expression of Christian monotheism and prevented from lapsing into a kind of Christ-ism in which the essential oneness of God is, after all, fragmented into a kind of bi-theism or tri-theism.

2 THE BIRTH NARRATIVES

As is well known, the first two chapters of the Gospels of both Matthew and Luke tell the story of Jesus' birth. There are many different elements and angles in the two accounts, but both focus on the same claim – the virgin birth of Jesus. Or to be more precise, the conception of Jesus by Mary when she was still virgin. In Matthew's account Joseph realizes that Mary his betrothed is pregnant before they have had intercourse, but is prevented from divorcing her by an angel who addresses him as 'Joseph, son of David', and assures him (1.20) that

'that which is conceived in her is of the Holy Spirit',

thus fulfilling the prophecy of Isaiah 7.14 (1.23) –

'Behold, a virgin shall conceive and bear a son,
and his name shall be called Emmanuel' (which means, God with us).

In Luke Mary is told by an angel prior to her pregnancy that she will conceive and bear a son (1.32-5):

He will be great, and will be called the Son of the Most High;
and the Lord God will give to him the throne of his father David,
and he will reign over the house of Jacob for ever;
and of his kingdom there will be no end.

The Holy Spirit will come upon you,
and the power of the Most High will overshadow you;
therefore the child to be born will be called holy,
the Son of God.

Here the issues are even more sensitive. What is involved is not merely a Pauline passage over which there was some controversy in the third and fourth centuries, but an element of the NT account of Jesus which has become a fixed part of Christian faith – the credal affirmation made by all Christians that Jesus was 'conceived by the Holy Spirit' and 'born of the Virgin Mary'. What room is there for dialogue here?

Nevertheless, dialogue there has to be. For when the attempt is made once again to set these passages back into their original context an element of unclarity and some questioning emerges. The key issue is the status of the birth narratives themselves: Were they intended as straightforward historical narratives or as something else? And if the latter, how much of them was intended to provide historical fact? Once again it has to be stressed that to raise such questions is not to deny or discard the subsequent credal affirmations. Rather, as with the case of Col. 1.15–20, it is a matter of checking to see how fully and how clearly the subsequent statements of the Creed succeeded in expressing the claim being made by the two Gospel writers.

On this subject the concerns of both scholarship and faith have been greatly assisted by the work of Raymond Brown. A Catholic scholar who prizes both words ('Catholic' and 'scholar'), his various writings and comments on the virginal conception of Jesus display a very fine-tuned form of the dialogue of NT theology. In his major study, *The Birth of the Messiah*,[1] a very careful exegetical analysis results in the following historical conclusions. (1) Lying behind both accounts, of Matthew and Luke, is the earlier Christian conviction that Jesus was God's Son begotten through the Holy Spirit. Also the tradition of an angelic annunciation of the birth of the Davidic Messiah. Already in the pre-Gospel tradition on which both Matthew and Luke drew, these two emphases had been combined – Jesus as 'son of David', but also, and more important, 'Son of God'. (2) The tradition of Jesus' Davidic descent seems to be well-grounded: it seems always to be taken for granted and never to have been seriously questioned; and the alternative messianic claim of priestly descent from Levi or Aaron seems never even to have been considered. (3) The prophecy of Isa. 7.14 used by Matthew ('a virgin shall conceive...') most probably did *not* give rise to the Christian belief in Mary's virginal conception of Jesus, but, at most, coloured the expression of an already existing Christian belief.

On the grounds of the same meticulous historical exegesis, however, other elements of the birth narratives produce a rather different impression. (4) Birth at Bethlehem becomes historically uncertain: there is no corroborating evidence for the two accounts anywhere else in the NT; and there is positive evidence that Nazareth and Galilee were regarded as Jesus' home town and native region. (5) Luke's report of a census under Quirinius during the reign of Herod the Great is almost certainly historically inaccurate. There *was* a census conducted by Quirinius, but that was of Judea (not of Galilee) and took place in AD 6–7.

Whether in some confusion of dates (cf. Acts 5.36–7) or deliberately, Luke has used a misdated event to explain the move from Nazareth to Bethlehem, so that Jesus' birth could take place in the latter. (6) A number of elements of the birth narratives can be described as 'midrashic', at least in the sense that they are modelled on and developed from OT texts and personages, rather than derived as a whole from historical data. In Luke's account Zechariah, Elizabeth, Simeon and Anna seem to be modelled on Abraham, Sarah, the parents of Samuel and Eli. And in Matthew's account the story about the magi from the east and the star is probably modelled in large measure on that of Balaam in Num.22—24 (with its prophecy of a star rising from Jacob, 24.17); while 'the slaughter of the innocents' is probably modelled on the Exodus 1 account of a pharaoh who commanded that all the male children of the Israelites should be killed.

We do not need to go into these matters in more detail, as would be necessary in the sort of full-scale exegesis Brown has given us. In fact his conclusions would be regarded as fairly conservative by many scholars. The point however is that his careful study shows there to be a strong likelihood, on exegetical grounds, that the narratives of Jesus' conception and birth are not to be taken as straightforward history, in large part at least. This means that we today should take care not to read the birth narratives of Matthew and Luke in terms of our own canons of historiography, where precision and accuracy of detail is at a premium. We must rather learn to read them in terms of ancient historiography, where a greater degree of artistic freedom was not merely permitted but expected and prized. Or perhaps even in terms of good story-telling, where elaboration of a given theme with richly embroidered details was the art of the genre. That is to say, if it is indeed the case that the Evangelists, and their tradition, used such artistic devices, as seems likely, we have to conclude that they did not intend to record what *we* call straightforward history. And, equally important, their initial readership, fully conversant with the genre being employed, would have read and understood the narratives in that light, and not as a detailed portrayal of actual events.

In other words we may be forced to conclude that the birth narratives of Matthew and Luke are more accurately to be likened to the modern historical novel – using authentic historical colour and historically plausible settings, but with freedom in detail to make a claim in terms which the intended readers would understand and whose character they would appreciate. But if that is the case, then for us today to insist that the narratives should be taken as straightforward historical accounts is to *mis*hear and *mis*understand them – at least in the way they were intended to be heard and understood. Indeed, so to insist (that they must be taken as factually accurate history) would be to abuse and distort their intended meaning and message.

What then of the central claim itself, central at least as encapsulated by the Creed – the virginal conception by the Spirit and virgin birth from Mary? Here again the possibility cannot be ruled out that these details too are part of the early Christian way of expressing the claim that Jesus was not only son of David but also Son of God, and was so from conception and birth. Exegetically the position is not so clear as in either of the sets of examples listed above, (1) to (3), or (4) to (6). On the one hand, there is the absence of any indication of awareness of a tradition of miraculous birth in the other earliest Christian traditions. On the few occasions that Mary appears in the other Gospels there is no hint that she herself retained such a memory (Mark 3.31–5; John 2.3–4). And on the other, there is at least a suggestion that during Jesus' life there was some public awareness of something unusual or irregular about Jesus' birth, which became the basis for a charge of illegitimacy. Note Mark 6.3 (to call someone the son of his mother implies that his father was not known and that he was illegitimate) and John 8.41 (the Jews' protest, 'We were not born illegitimate'). Brown himself concludes 'that the *scientifically controllable* biblical evidence leaves the question of the historicity of the virginal conception unresolved'.[2]

At the same time there is plenty of evidence that the portrayal of someone regarded as very special by presenting his birth as something supernatural was a well established and well accepted convention of the time. Such heroes as Romulus, Alexander and Augustus were all depicted with poetic hyperbole as descended from the gods. And in Jewish tradition the birth of Isaac when both Abraham and Sarah were past childbearing was well known (Gen. 17.17; Rom. 4.19), and indeed may have provided the model for Luke's description of the birth of John the Baptist

(Luke 1.18). Likewise the model of angelic annunciation of a birth before it happened – Ishmael (Gen. 16.7–13), Samson (Judg. 13.3–5) and again John the Baptist (Luke 1.11–20). There is nothing quite like the Gospels' accounts of virginal conception, of course, but it would hardly have been unexpected that Christians should formulate the distinctiveness of their claim in distinctive terms. At this point the decisive consideration may not be the details used but the genre in which the claim was made. At all events, so far as exegesis is concerned, the possibility remains open that the account of the virginal conception of Jesus was intended not as a description of historical fact but as a Christian variant on the convention that the origin of epochally significant figures should be presented in supernatural terms.

It should be stated clearly that such possibilities can be considered without, as a necessary consequence, calling in question the inspiration and authority of the scriptural texts involved. On the contrary, the whole motivation of a historically oriented exegesis is to hear the scriptural text in its original terms, to hear what the author intended to say, to hear what the original readers heard the Spirit say to them through it. The insistence that a text can be heard with only one of the meanings within a broader range of meaning which the author intended is not to defend or safeguard the inspiration and authority of the text, but to impose on the text a criterion of judgement drawn from outside it and usually considerably subsequent to it. If an author wrote within both the constraints and liberty of current idiom and genre, then we do him most respect when we hear him in those terms, even if it means that we cannot, as in this case, assert a clear-cut dogmatic conclusion from what he has written.

All we have done so far is to clarify one pole and one voice within the dialogue on this subject – that the virginal conception and birth of Jesus are not certainly historical facts, and a literal understanding of them may not be the surely intended meaning of the authors. That they intended their readers to believe that Jesus was the son of David and Son of God from the beginning of his time on earth is clear. But that they presented this claim in midrashic, or symbolical, or poetic form, rather than as straightforward historical fact, is quite probable, and certainly cannot be ruled out.

But when the dialogue proceeds what difference does it make? Has the NT in its original meaning completely fixed the agenda for the continuing dialogue and its outcome? The subsequent development of Christian dogma would say No! In its wisdom the Church came to the conclusion that the birth narratives should after all be regarded as describing hard historical fact. We can put the point more precisely: the Church through its authoritative statements, universally recognized as such by more or less all Christian traditions, has ruled that a view of the birth narratives, which may not be firmly grounded in historical exegesis or be in full accord with the mind of the original authors, is after all the faith of the Church. This is where Raymond Brown clearly states his position as not just a NT scholar, but a *Catholic* scholar.[3] He recognizes that in the birth narratives all the details are not historical, and that the view that Jesus' divine sonship stems from a virginal conception is a minority NT view. But he also strongly asserts that the Church has eliminated the ambiguity and uncertainty of the biblical narratives and has provided the authoritative interpretation of these texts.

But is that wholly satisfactory? Does it give sufficient weight to the *sola scriptura* of Reformation protest over against the more Catholic view of the development of doctrine? Does it actually allow dialogue to proceed, or does it in effect confine the dialogue of theology to one between current questioners and the *creeds* (rather than Scripture)? Does it sufficiently allow the original scriptural text to criticize the subsequent formulations – to fulfil its canonical role? Moreover, does it take sufficient account of the fact that the credal statements are themselves historically contingent – answering questions which were posed within a different conceptuality, with answers which belong within that conceptuality but which now have in turn themselves to be translated if they are to have the same effect now as then? The transformation in the category of 'person', which is of equal importance in classic Christology but which certainly cannot simply be translated into our modern concept of 'person' without completely distorting catholic faith, is an indication of the problem. Indeed the dialogue of theology is liable to be most fruitful when it is realized that both biblical text *and* credal formula are trying to express something essentially inexpressible in human categories, since they are all too limited and restrictive. In other words, even in the creeds themselves 'the virgin birth' may have to be understood in terms of metaphor if the inexpressibility of the incarnation is not to be lost. If so, an exegete would have to say that such an understanding was probably a better reflection of the character of the birth narratives in the Gospels.

Here too, then, as with Col. 1.15-20, the question arises as to whether, in a debate about the incarnation where the concerns are the same but the conceptualities are different, it might not be more appropriate to dialogue directly with the original and seemingly more flexible scriptural texts. Not in disregard for the credal formulae, but in recognition that their tighter formulation may be less relevant to the different dialogue of the twentieth century and may in consequence actually obscure and confuse the doctrine of the incarnation for us today rather than clarify or defend it.

3   JOHN 14.6

5 Thomas said to him (Jesus): 'Lord, we do not know where you are going; how can we know the way?' 6 Jesus said to him: 'I am the way, and the truth, and the life; no one comes to the Father, but by me.'

With this text another central aspect of Christian beliefs and claims regarding Jesus Christ comes to the fore. Not just the uniqueness of Christ (also evident in the previous passages), but also the *exclusivity* of the claims made. If it is indeed the fact that the only way to God is through Christ, then the claim of any other religion is at once put in question and radically discounted. All alternative claims to insight into divine reality are thereby diminished if not wholly denied; and all other claims to provide a way of salvation are thereby dismissed as false and delusive. Is this what the text intended or requires? Not least of the problems which attend such a sweeping assertion is that it seems to cut short any dialogue before it has even started. The exclusivity of the claim made for Christ in John 14.6 seems to be of the take-it-or-leave-it variety, allowing no room for debate or compromise. What contribution can a historical exegesis make in a case like this? Is there any room for the dialogue of NT theology?

One aspect of the issue can be dealt with fairly quickly. Few scholars today would regard the saying in John 14.6 as words uttered by Jesus himself during his earthly ministry. This conclusion is a particular case in point of a more general observation regarding the discourses of Jesus in John's Gospel as a whole. They were almost certainly *not* intended as historical transcripts of Jesus' teaching. It is much more likely that they were shaped and produced as meditations or sermons on aspects of Jesus' ministry (including particular deeds and words), *and* that they would have been understood as such by the first readers of John's Gospel. The case for this conclusion is made in detail in most modern commentators. I have highlighted its most obvious and persuasive features in *The Evidence for Jesus*[4] and need not rehearse it again at any length here.

Two of the most important considerations are in fact exemplified in our text. (1) The prominence of Father/Son language in the Fourth Gospel. This *far* exceeds anything we find in the other three Gospels. In particular Jesus' talk of 'the Father' (as here): in Mark, only once; in the 'Q' material, only once; in the material peculiar to Matthew, only once; in the material peculiar to Luke, only twice; but in John the phrase appears on Jesus' lips no less than 73 times! The most obvious conclusion is that this is an elaborated theme in John – not created or invented by the Fourth Evangelist, but certainly elaborated (otherwise the contrast with the other three Gospels could hardly have been so marked). And this must mean, in turn, that most of the 'the Father' sayings in John are, strictly speaking, unhistorical in the sense that Jesus himself did not say them. This may say nothing about the truth claim involved in these sayings, but that is another question to which we must return. For the moment it is sufficient to draw the historical exegetical conclusion that John 14.6 is more likely to express John's view of Jesus than Jesus' view of himself.

(2) John 14.6 is, of course, one of the famous 'I am' sayings of Jesus – the others being 'I am the bread of life' (6.35, 48); 'I am the light of the world' (8.12); 'I am the door' (10.7, 9); 'I am the good shepherd' (10.11, 14); 'I am the resurrection and the life' (11.25); and 'I am the true vine' (15.1, 5). There is also

the even more striking 8.58, 'Before Abraham was I am'. The point is that these sayings occur *only* in John's Gospel. It is scarcely credible that sayings like this would have been so totally ignored by the other Evangelists had they been available to them. The much more obvious and pressing conclusion is that they did *not* belong to the tradition of Jesus' sayings from the beginning. Rather they are a particularly vivid and expressive way of bringing out the significance of Jesus – a literary device, if you like. As such they became a feature of the peculiarly Johannine portrayal of Jesus, and may have helped to shape that portrayal as well as to express it. Again the issue here is simply that of *when* such formulations appeared, not the question of whether they are true. Indeed, we may very well and properly want to maintain that these sayings express what those who shaped the Johannine tradition found Jesus to be in their experience of the gospel and of faith. But the point here is that the Jesus who comes thus to expression in a saying like John 14.6 is not simply the Jesus of AD 30 in Galilee or Jerusalem, but that Jesus reflected on over some years and experienced as ascended Lord.

(3) A similar point can be made about a further feature of the text – Jesus' talk of 'the truth'. Here too the contrast with the other three Gospels is striking. In *none* of them does Jesus speak of 'the truth' – not once. But in the Fourth Gospel the phrase appears repeatedly on his lips – no less than twenty-two times. Here again it would be disingenuous to argue in the face of such evidence that, after all, Jesus himself did speak frequently of 'the truth'. The language must be evidence of a developed view of Jesus seen through a prism of faith and truth experienced. At the same time, we may well have here a good example of how that development proceeded. For in all three other Gospels we have recorded an assessment of Jesus which has striking parallel to John 14.6: the Pharisees who endeavour to entrap Jesus by flattering him – 'In truth you teach the way of God' (Matt. 22.16; Mark 12.14; Luke 20.21). It is quite likely that those who shaped the Johannine tradition knew this Synoptic exchange and transformed the words of flattery into a truth claim of Jesus himself.

Two relevant points emerge here. The first is that John 14.6 is a claim made *for* Jesus rather than a claim made *by* Jesus during his time on earth. Once again we have to insist that such a finding does not necessarily affect the truth of that claim. In other words, the truth claim of John 14.6 is not dependent on whether Jesus actually said these words or not – and to make that truth claim depend on an unjustifiably narrow understanding of John's intention would be both to undermine and distort it. In theological terms we may still say that Jesus was who he was even if he did not say anything about it; Jesus was who John claimed he was even if he himself did not know it. Which is also to remind ourselves that John's presentation is also part of Scripture. However it emerged, John 14.6 is still a scriptural assertion.

Second, we should appreciate the fact that we have in the above discussion a good example of the point made in Chapter 1, that the dialogue of NT theology is already present within the NT itself. Whenever we meet a text behind which lies some tradition and some developing insight or interpretation we have a text which is a product of that dialogue. In this case between the remembered ministry and preaching of Jesus and the full significance of his ministry as a whole (including his death and resurrection) as increasingly perceived by (some) first-century Christians in terms of their own conceptuality and in relation to the concerns and questions of their own day.

The above discussion is an important part of the total dialogue of NT theology. But in one sense it is more like a ground clearing exercise opening up the more important question for the dialogue as a whole. That question focuses on the truth claim of John 14.6 itself rather than on its literary prehistory. What is it that John 14.6 claims about Jesus? What was it that the person who gave the Fourth Gospel its definitive character and shape intended his readers to hear and believe on the basis of this text? In order to answer this question the task of historical exegesis must turn from traditio-historical analysis to an investigation of the function of John 14.6 within the Gospel. What was the context in which and to which John was speaking when he wrote 14.6? What wider assumptions were in play, but unspoken, but which nevertheless would have influenced his formulation and how it was heard? To carry through such an investigation thoroughly would require more space than we have here. But it may be sufficient to expand a little on three important aspects

(1) The claim for the uniqueness and exclusivity of Jesus in John 14.6 is of a piece with the traditional Jewish claim for the uniqueness and exclusivity of their God. One of the fundamental 'taken-for-granteds' within Jewish and earliest Jewish Christian writing was the conviction that God is one – monotheism. For centuries Judaism had been confronted by a wide range of polytheistic belief. Surrounding nations and cultures were able to function with the concept of many gods (cf. 1 Cor. 8.6, 'gods many' and 'lords many'). More sophisticated was the widespread syncretism of the Hellenistic world, where the gods of different traditions were seen as the same god and different gods could be seen as manifestations of a single divine power. So Zeus and Jupiter were different names for the same god. Or the Greek goddess Minerva could be identified with the local British Sul (at Bath). Or Isis could be called 'the many-named' because many different gods were seen as manifestations of her.

We know what happened when these other more widespread systems came into conflict with Jewish belief. The Maccabean crisis was caused by the attempt of the Syrian king to impose the typical Hellenistic belief that Yahweh was simply the local name for Olympian Zeus (2 Macc. 6.2). Jews were often regarded as atheists, not because of their monotheism, but because they were unwilling to recognize other gods as manifestations of deity equivalent to their own. And where Jew and Gentile lived side by side amicably in the diaspora it was common to speak of the Jewish God simply as 'God Most High' (on the parallel of Zeus Most High). The characteristic Jewish reaction was to insist all the more fiercely on the unparalleled majesty of their God (Second Isaiah gives it classic expression). The gods of other nations, if they had existence at all, were simply angels, part of the one God's heavenly retinue and subordinates (as in Job 1—2; Jubilees 15.31). The creed of Deut. 6.4 should continue to be said by the devout Jew night and morning – 'The Lord our God is one Lord', or 'The Lord our God, the Lord is one'.

It is in the context of this fundamental Jewish axiom that John 14.6 should be read. The uniqueness claimed for Jesus in John 14.6, over against other claimants to revelatory and salvific significance, is parallel to and probably in part at least expressive of the classic Jewish claim that God is one, over against all other claims to deity in the wider world.

(2) Belief in divine wisdom is caught up in all this. As we saw above (on Col. 1. 15–20), Wisdom could readily be perceived as a distinct divine being in the other systems surrounding Judaism. Or in terms of the syncretism just described, 'Wisdom' could serve, for example, as one of the goddess Isis' many names. But, as we also saw, the Jewish wisdom writers in adopting such or similar language domesticated it within Judaism and contained it within their monotheistic axiom – Wisdom as a personification of God in his dealings with his world and his people, Wisdom as the face of God turned towards his creation.

The most striking and far-reaching expression of this domestication was the identification of wisdom with the law (Ecclus. 24.23; Baruch 4.1). The claim was bold. The divine wisdom which was far beyond the capacity of man to find for himself (Job 28) had been given to Israel (Baruch 3). The divine wisdom which penetrated all things (Wisd. 7.24) had been focused in the Torah. The divine female figure appealing for a hearing in Proverbs had been identified with a book.

All this has to be borne in mind when we read John's Gospel. For John has taken up the same imagery and identified it with Christ. In the prologue (John 1.1–18) he takes up the equivalent concept of the word (Logos) and speaks of its pre-incarnation history in the sort of language typical of Jewish talk of wisdom. The point comes to sharpest expression towards the end of the prologue, when he insists that the fulness of grace has come through Christ, not the law: 'the law was given through Moses; grace and truth came through Jesus Christ' (1.17). In other words, John is saying here to those who have hitherto seen the law as the pre-eminent expression of divine wisdom that Christ has now superseded the law in that role. Christ is the fullest and final embodiment of God's Word and Wisdom. So too in the rest of the Gospel much of the imagery used for Christ is taken over in large part from the earlier Jewish talk of wisdom. The 'I am' statements, of which 14.6 is one, include some of the best examples, since it is just in such first person terms and with such imagery that divine wisdom often spoke in the Jewish wisdom tradition.

In short, here too we cannot understand the point John is making in 14.6 unless we bear in mind two important background factors. The first is that John, like the Jewish wisdom

writers before him, is drawing on a much more cosmic or universal concept of divine interaction with the world when he
paints his portrait of Jesus in wisdom colours. And the second
is that John is doing so in dialogue and dispute with other
Jewish writers who had already been doing something the same
with the law for some time. That is to say, the uniqueness and
exclusivity claimed for Jesus in John 14.6 is intended to provide
a very specific rebuttal both of widespread non-Jewish claims
that divine wisdom could be found equally in a whole variety of
religious and philosophical systems, and of strongly held Jewish
claims that divine wisdom was located exclusively in the law.

(3) One other feature of John's presentation should not go
without mention. For also characteristic of his Gospel is the
portrayal of the gospel choice in stark and blunt terms. Hence
the frequently observed antitheses between light and darkness,
death and life, truth and error, etc. (see e.g. 1.5, 3.19–21; 5.24;
8.12, 44–5; 9.39–41). This does not necessarily mean that the
Evangelist himself saw issues in rather simplified, black and
white terms – though that certainly is very possible. It may
simply mean that in order to compel his readers to make crucial
choices he felt it necessary to pose them in as sharp and uncompromising terms as possible (so also in 1 John, e.g. 2.4, 23;
3.6, 9–10, 14–15; 4.5–6).

In other words, it is not simply the Christology of John 14.6
which is uncompromising in the demands it makes on John's
readers. This is part of an evangelistic or paraenetic strategy to
force his readers to recognize the either-or of faith in Christ
which confronts them (cf. 20.31). This strongly suggests that
14.6 should not be read simply as a dogmatic definition; it has
been given its exclusivist note not to serve as a credal statement
but for the particular task of bringing the recipients of the
document to the decision of faith.

When we take these factors into account in the dialogue which
focuses on and stems from John 14.6 we become aware that the
meaning of the text, both past and present, is not quite so
straightforward as at first appeared. (a) We have to recognize
again the force of John's wisdom Christology, as in the case of
Col. 1.15–20. The exclusiveness which John claims for Christ is
the exclusiveness both of the Jewish claim that God is one and
of the Christian claim that that one God has expressed himself/

herself in the man Christ Jesus in as full a way as it was possible
for a human being to embody/incarnate God. (b) We have to
recognize that the exclusiveness claimed for Jesus as the revelation of God and way to God is set particularly in antithesis to
the similar Jewish claim for the Torah.

(c) At the same time however, we have to recognize that
wisdom was also conceived of as a power which pervades the
cosmos, even though unknown to and undiscoverable by human
beings by their own unaided effort. God's wisdom and active
presence pervades the world, even when it comes to focus in
Torah or Christ. In other words, what we have in wisdom
theology is not an exclusiveness which denies God's presence
anywhere else, but an exclusiveness which gives a means of
recognizing it elsewhere.

So in John 1, the Logos is 'the light which shines in the
darkness,...the true light which enlightens every man' (1.5, 9).
And that still remains a true description of the Word of God,
even when it has come to particular and final focus in the flesh
of Jesus (1.14). Even with John himself, the incarnation of the
Logos does not exclude the complementary idea of the one God's
creative, revealing and saving action more widespread in the
world. And that insight seems to find confirmation from point
(3) above: the out-and-outness of the claim made in 14.6 is in
large part at least a way of drawing attention to the significance
of Jesus – an evangelistic rather than a dogmatic exclusivity of
claim. In other words, here too the exclusiveness of the claim
made for Christ may simply be a way of indicating that Christ
is now the clearest pattern and model of divine action in the
world, the norm by which other claims to express such divine
action may be measured.

(d) In recognizing that the Christian claim for Christ as the
embodiment of wisdom was put in some opposition to the equivalent Jewish claim for the Torah, we must also recall that it
was part of a larger Christian protest against Jewish exclusivism.
It was precisely the claim that God was God of the Jews only,
as evidenced not least by his giving them the Torah, which
Christians found necessary to question. Paul argued the point
very deftly, on the basis of the Jewish premise of monotheism.
'Is God the God of Jews only? Is he not the God of Gentiles

also? Yes, of Gentiles also, since God is one...' (Rom. 3.29–30). In breaching the walls of Jewish exclusivism it is not so likely that the first Christians would have understood the Johannine Christ to assert a new exclusivism. The sharpness of John's antitheses certainly lends some credibility to the suggestion, but as we have seen, that sharpness is probably as much a homiletic device as anything.

The danger, however, is that a too uncontextualized reading of John 14.6 will result in just the sort of exclusivism that Christianity began by rejecting. Christ is no longer on earth, the embodiment of God's wisdom and word confined by geographical location. As ascended, he now fills the cosmic role previously filled by Wisdom and Spirit. The danger is that, despite his exaltation, he becomes imprisoned in the Church or in dogma, in the same way that wisdom was confined within the Torah. Once again this is not to deny John 14.6, so much as to point out that the Wisdom-Christ, who is the self-expression of the God of all, cannot be restricted within creed or ecclesiastical structure. He is God!

When we thus engage in the exegetical part of the dialogue of NT theology, we begin to see that the claim in John 14.6 may not be so exclusive or so dismissive of other claimants to divine revelation and salvation as at first appeared. The uniqueness claimed for Christ may simply be a way of saying that Jesus is the normative expression of God. The exclusiveness claimed for Christ may simply be a way of bringing home the strength and urgency of that claim in a world full of alternative and enticing mediators and deities. That seems to be the primary thrust of the Johannine claim, not the outright denial that God's Spirit and word may well be experienced elsewhere in the world. It would certainly constitute an unchristian narrowing of the gospel if it were to be denied that the Word of God was never heard or Spirit of God never experienced outside an explicitly Christian context. Properly understood, John 14.6 does not in fact exclude the idea that God may be at work in hearts or situations, even where the name of Christ has never been heard. If love is the chief fruit of the Spirit, then wherever love is there is the Spirit – that is, the Spirit of Christ. If wisdom is the gift of heavenly Wisdom, then wherever true wisdom is known there is Wisdom-Christ. John 14.6 allows plenty of room for the hidden or unselfconscious Christian.

At the same time John 14.6 does indicate that Christ is the touchstone by which heavenly love and divine wisdom may be recognized. It is by the yardstick of Christ, *not* the dogmas about Christ, that the unknown Christian may be recognized. For Christians, certainly, to claim that Christ is the fullest and normative expression of God is not to prevent but rather to facilitate the awareness of God's grace in its wider manifestations. All this is also to say that the dialogue of theology cannot be an exclusively internal Christian dialogue, but must also be open to all truth and salvation claims, even if Christians will still want to bring them all to the test of Christ, God's saving outreach in human flesh.

NOTES

1 R. Brown, *The Birth of the Messiah* (London, Chapman, 1977).
2 *Birth*, p. 527.
3 e.g. in his *Biblical Exegesis and Church Doctrine* (London, Chapman, 1986), pp. 35–7.
4 J. D. G. Dunn, *The Evidence for Jesus* (London, SCM, 1985).

4

First Test Case: Christology
(2) A View from Systematic Theology

Coincidences make history; they make the history of theology too – and that in its own way illustrates our contention about the contextualization of all texts, the historical conditioning of all theology and of all of its doctrinal distillations.

When the first draft of the previous chapter by my collaborator arrived on my desk, John Hick was already here in Edinburgh to deliver the Gifford Lectures, and he had just conducted a seminar in the Faculty of Divinity on what he saw to be the most crucial problem in contemporary Christology. Briefly stated, this was the problem of constructing *and* making acceptable to Christians generally the kind of Christology which could serve as the basis for an authentically theocentric development of Christianity, and which could in consequence be a help rather than a hindrance to people who increasingly experience religious pluralism.[1] Those who keep themselves *au courant* with his recent publications will know how Hick has been concerned for some years past with the production of a Christian theology of religions which would not include any pre-emptive claims to Christian superiority, much less encourage that kind of exclusivism which had to pretend that all other religions were false and hence inherently idolatrous.[2]

In the seminar just mentioned Hick had assumed that the dominant form of traditional Christology, Chalcedonian Christology as it is sometimes called, inevitably entailed pre-emptive claims to the unchallengeable superiority of the Christian religion, even if it did not inevitably entail exclusivist attitudes. He was then anxious to promote alternative Christologies which could point Christians to the one God, without invidious implications for other religious traditions in the world that are, each in its own way, trying to do the same thing.

It was impossible for me during the seminar to avoid being struck by the coincidence with a theme which emerges so powerfully towards the end of the previous chapter: the argument that texts of Scripture concerning Jesus the Christ which might at first sight seem exclusivist in the extreme, serve in fact to counteract a Jewish exclusivism, and positively point towards, rather than deny, the salvific presence of something of God in the world at large. Even if I had been tempted to seek another angle on the systematician's view of the dialogue, within Christology, between Scripture and dogma, this coincidence would surely have prevented me. As things turned out, I was reminded that in Chapter 2 I had placed Christology amongst the essential doctrines of the faith which are no longer a matter of dispute between major Christian bodies, and which therefore require of us, if we are ever to understand their cultural/historical conditioning, to pay the closest attention to this widest cultural context within which these doctrines develop. The coincidence reminds me that the most obvious feature of contemporary culture – most obvious, at least, for development of doctrine – is the growing awareness of the religious pluralism of the race, made even more persistently evident by our sense of a shrinking globe. The angle from which as a systematician I must view the dialogue of Scripture and dogma concerning Christology, then, is the angle offered by the converging claims of the world religions.

1 THE SUPERIORITY OF DOGMA

Here is Hick's statement of the present problem with Chalcedonian Christology. The fifth-century Council of Chalcedon declared 'that the one selfsame Christ, only-begotten Son and Lord, must be acknowledged in two natures ... that the specific character of each nature is preserved, and they are united in one person and one 'hypostasis'; the Council at the same time declared that in his divine nature (as distinct from his human nature) Christ was 'one in substance' with the Father. We are to take it then, it would seem, that God is present 'in substance'

in human form as Jesus of Nazareth, in union with the fully
human nature of Jesus of Nazareth. In substance, not in mere
appearance or manifestation. Or, since the Greek word for substance (*ousia*) can be translated either by 'substance' or by
'being', the unique divine substance, wholly other and immutable when contrasted to changeable and interchangeable
creaturely substance, is present in and as Jesus the Lord; the
Divine Being itself is incarnate in Jesus.

From this particular incarnational Christology which found
its definitive expression at the Council of Chalcedon – for other
Christologies, as we shall see, can equally be called incarnational
– Hick draws the following implication, and in doing so he is
reflecting a common consensus. The implication is that we are
now speaking of an intersection of the divine and the human
which occurs, *by definition*, only in this unique case. We are
therefore speaking of a unique superiority of Jesus which follows
with iron logic from this particular incarnational Christology,
and we can neither relinquish a consequent Christian claim to
superiority over other religions, nor can we regard that claim as
one which might be proved or disproved in the course of history
or by historical/comparative investigation.

If the Divine Being itself, in its own unique and absolute
substance is in Jesus, then Jesus is by that very fact superior to
all other religious leaders or founders in whom the presence of
the Divinity might be claimed, and allowed to be in some degree
manifest. Further, this common consensus would lead us to
believe, this kind of Christology would forever set the followers
of Jesus above the rest of humanity in a religiously pluralistic
world, and require of all other religions that they finally convert
to Jesus on penalty of otherwise missing the fulness of truth.
Here, then, is a case of officially formulated dogma which appears to pre-empt in one important respect that openness to
broader culture which Chapter 2 required. Here is a good test
case for the conviction, expressed in Chapter 2 that cultivated
awareness of broader cultural contexts for theological doctrines
could help the process of discovering the scriptural horizon, by
bringing its own quorum of awareness to the work of the
exegete. For the exegete is also intent upon discovering the
scriptural horizon within the fusion of horizons which make up
both the exegete's and the systematician's consciousness at any

one time. The characteristic contribution of the systematician to the ensuing dialogue must be the critical analysis of, in this case, the Chalcedonian dogma, in increased awareness of broad cultural categories and movements. To this critical analysis I now turn.

First, it might be worth noting, since comparative religion is now our context, that claims quite similar to those officially formulated at Chalcedon are made in other religions for other religious leaders. John Hick, in the paper under consideration here, gave the example of a developing Buddhist belief – which, as in the case of its Christian comparator, took almost five centuries to complete – that the Buddha Gautama had a supernatural conception, birth and childhood, and that he was in fact 'God beyond the gods' or 'God of gods', something equivalent to the Western concept of the most perfect Divine Being, incarnate. What is striking about this developed Buddhology of early Mahayana Buddhism is not merely its close similarity to Chalcedonian Christology, but the fact that this Buddhology was apparently not thought to be in the least incompatible with many incarnations, many Buddhas living human lives in this world at different times. Are we to assume that these early Buddhist theologians, blinded perhaps by general beliefs in reincarnation, failed to see the logic of uniqueness which our common Christian consensus attempts to bring to everyone's attention? Or is the logic of the Christian consensus itself faulty? Does the presence in human form of the very Divine Being itself logically entail one, and only one incarnation?

It would seem to me to be quite impossible to answer that question as it stands, for to answer it as it stands we should have to be able to take a God's-eye view of the matter. That is to say, we should have to know or to pretend to know, so much about the Divine Being in itself that we could *see* the intrinsic impossibility of its assuming a human nature more than once. But we cannot take the God's-eye view. Our gaze, as the poet said, is submarine. We look upwards and catch as much of the refracted light as our mortal eyes can bear, and if we know anything at all about the Light in itself, the light at Source, it is that it is incalculably greater than any of its shinings which in this life and this world we are capable of seeing. Hence the presence in

Chapter 3 of what might be called qualifying phrases: 'in as full a way as it was possible for a human being to embody/ incarnate God'. For it is everywhere recognized, in the Christian tradition in any case, that the presence of the Divine Being in human form or in any created nature, involves *kenosis*, self-emptying, a voluntary humiliation, a divine condescension.

If we were capable of seeing Divine Substance in itself, or thought that we had seen it in itself rather than in the form of the human and the creaturely, we might be able to mount a logical argument from the absoluteness of the Divine Being to the absoluteness of one incarnation. But when we talk, as it seems we must, of Divine Being incarnate 'in as full a way as possible' no such argument is immediately obvious. In fact given the enormous variety in the human form across cultures and in the long course of human history, there might well be an antecedent expectation that the Divine Being would have become incarnate 'in as full a way as possible' in more than a few individuals. But that kind of argument would be as speculative as the other, and both would return us once more to the existence of incarnational claims, and counterclaims, and to the need to find some way of assessing these, rather than merely making them.

Secondly, then, one must turn a critical eye on the term 'incarnation' itself. Christians have a habit of speaking of 'The Incarnation'. By this they convey the impression, not only that there was but one incarnation, but that the term refers to the first instant of the conception of Jesus in the womb of Mary. That conception was 'the incarnation'. Now this mode of ref erence in fact deprives the word 'nature' used at Chalcedon of most of its native force. For 'nature' (*physis*) is a dynamic rather than a static concept. Like 'substance' it denotes a thing. But whereas 'substance' connotes that aspect of things whereby they subsist, support and sustain, 'nature' connotes the characteristic way in which a particular thing acts, behaves, or lives. For God to 'be acknowledged' in a human *physis* then, we should have to think of the Divine Being living a characteristically human life, and incarnation would have to apply to that whole life in all its historical concreteness, rather than to some abstract moment of conception. In this respect at least Chalcedon, properly understood, brings us close to the Scriptures in which God's presence is confessed in all of Jesus' life, death and destiny, for all of that belongs to a human 'nature'.

It follows that we really must reject quite firmly those rather crude distinctions so frequently forced between incarnational and adoptionist Christologies as they are called, distinctions which seem to coincide with others, such as those between physical and adoptive divine sonship, or between metaphysical and metaphorical attribution of divine sonship. For all these seem to take the life, death and destiny of Jesus which was and still is part of this world's history, and to look elsewhere for the content of the doctrines proposed. So, for example the 'physical' Son of God to whom sonship may be attributed 'metaphysically' is a pre-existent divine person in some sense analogous to the way in which we are persons (and then, as Chapter 3 pointed out, we are polytheists). This 'physical' Son then, of course, becomes incarnate at the moment of Jesus' conception, and that is then 'the incarnation'. On the contrary, any Christology which looked to the human life, death and resurrection of Jesus and described in terms of spirit ('God is spirit') the presence in all of this of the Divine Being, would be described as adoptionist, the ensuing sonship adoptive, and its attribution merely metaphorical. There simply is no justification for such invidious value judgements. Of course, in the history of Christology there were, and no doubt there are still, heretical examples of the *genre*, but these cannot be detected, much less corrected, by the crude method of categorizing which is all too unfortunate a feature of Christian theology.

Too much has been discovered, or rediscovered, recently about the heuristic power of metaphor and its ability to reveal the depths and heights of the real, to allow the term 'metaphorical' to be used in a pejorative sense. Chapter 3 on more than one occasion suggested that the richer and more flexible poetic imagery in which the Bible deals may serve our present purposes as Christian theologians better than dogmatic categories which have become more restrictive in their use. Indeed there is some evidence to suggest that the wish to define things in tight analytic categories often involves a kind of circular logic of power and exclusiveness. Like all drawing of a limit or boundary (*finis*), defining can serve to assert my control over the object concerned, whether it be territory or truth, and to exclude others from its enjoyment – except, of course, on my terms. A good deal of religious power-mongering follows this formula. But the power of analysis can also clarify parts of a richer imagery and test the implications of all of it; and it can even, when turned upon its own results, reveal their limitations, their limits, and in this use of itself become as liberating as other uses are restrictive and coercive. (For imagery, too, with its gentler power to evoke can sometimes, in the absence of thought taken, evoke quite the wrong, destructive response.)

So one might analyse more fully the common theological prejudice against what John Hick calls 'inspiration Christologies',[3] and which he prefers to Chalcedonian Christology on the grounds that they do not, as it does, secure the unique superiority of Jesus *by definition*.

One would find, I think, that whenever 'spirit' functions as a term for the Divine Being itself, or for the Divine Being insofar as it is powerfully present in human life or in the world, it is just as adequate a term as any other for use in a fully incarnational Christology. It is perfectly capable of saying all that the most fully incarnational Christology could wish to say, namely, that the Divine Being was present in this world by living a fully human life (by assuming, in other words, a fully human nature), at least to the extent that it is possible for a human being to 'incarnate' Divine Being. The only problem that can be caused by this manner of speech is a problem for traditional Christian Trinitarian theology, and not a problem for incarnational Christology. For it would then seem that we could say that the 'third' hypostasis of the Divinity which traditional Trinitarian theology names 'the Holy Spirit' was incarnate in Jesus of Nazareth; or alternatively we would have to evolve a 'binity' rather than a 'trinity' in which that which was incarnate in Jesus could be called equivalently Spirit or Son or Word. But that should not concern us here. At worst it would force on traditional Trinitarian doctrines the need to acknowledge that, like all doctrines, they are optional ways of expressing, without then confining, parts of a much richer tradition of theological wisdom. And it would do nothing to pre-empt the claims of traditional Trinitarian theology that for the looser language of the first three centuries should be substituted a theological rule or norm which would restrict to the terms Son or Word the expression of the presence of the Divine Being in Jesus of Nazareth, and use the term Spirit for the presence of the Divine Being, through Jesus, in the Church, and perhaps more broadly in the world.

For present purposes it is necessary only to note that 'inspiration Christologies' in their most substantial forms can be fully incarnational Christologies. The fact that some early inspirational Christologies were apparently flawed does not count against this contention; for other major Spirit Christologies, by Paul for example, expressed what later came to be called, more abstractly, the divinity of Jesus as adequately as any other (incarnational) Christology could manage to do. And some early Christologies in terms of 'Son' or 'Word' were even more obviously flawed than were Spirit Christologies.

Thirdly, then, this leads us to ask the central question: Did Chalcedon intend to say more than was said about God's presence in Jesus in the Scriptures? Or did it in fact say more than this? Here, really, is the crux of the matter. For whatever one might decide about similar-sounding claims in other religions to the effect that the Divine Being was present in human history in a particular person, and however strongly one might insist that in Christian theology at any rate Spirit-language is as adequate as is Word- or Son-language to the task of presenting such claims in their fulness, the dialogue of dogma and Scripture must still finally face this third question: Did Chalcedon say more than or, stronger still, something different from, what had already been claimed for divinity and Jesus in Scripture?

It has already been hinted in Chapter 2 that early Christian conflicts both with dominant non-Christian theologies and between developing Christian theologies tended to drive Christians in general towards a concept of deity more impassive and immutable than even a good Platonist would hold, and as a consequence towards a rather dualist view of Jesus, who suffered the contingencies of history in his humanity, but could not really suffer these in his 'divinity'. And this did much to spread the impression that in Jesus one was dealing with a Divine Person of altogether different structure and character from the human being with which he was somehow joined.

Early theology was clearly not altogether satisfied with this

scenario, for we find it seeking out ways in which to predicate of
Jesus' humanity the attributes of divinity, and of Jesus' divinity
the characteristic experiences of being human, including of
course the distinctively human experiences of suffering and
dying. This was done on the grounds that, after all, as Chalcedon
itself finally defined the matter, there was but one 'person' or
'hypostasis' present in Jesus of Nazareth. Actions and passions
are, in the end, of persons and so, irrespective of the 'nature'
which they prove to be present, they can all be predicated of the
one person. The person of divine nature could suffer, the person
of human nature raise a child from the dead, and provided we
acknowledge one selfsame Christ in two natures, and the unity,
the one-ness, to consist in this thing called 'person' or 'hypostasis', it is truly the one person of divine nature who suffers
and the selfsame person of human nature who performed
miracles.

Now it would be quite unfair to conclude that this rather
elaborate way of talking about Jesus was like closing the stable
door after the horse had gone; that it represented a despairing
attempt to reduce impressions of duality between an impassible
divinity and a very vulnerable human being, long after such
impressions had been very fully conveyed. To be fair to it, the
mainstream theological tradition had always tried its best to
preserve the full implications of incarnation, of the belief, that
is to say, that the Divine Being had become a human being, had
taken on a fully human nature, had lived a recognizably human
life and died a very human death.

The main problem lay with the word 'person'. The word had
been used in Trinitarian theology to speak about differentiation
within the Divine Being. Christians had always felt that there
was some distinction between God as Source of all and God as
present in Jesus (and elsewhere in the world). This corresponds
to the feeling that God is present in Jesus with the qualification
already mentioned: 'in as full a way as it was possible for a
human being to embody/incarnate God'. This qualification
does not of course imply that only a percentage of God is present
in Jesus – it was the rejected Arian view that the divinity present
in Jesus was something lesser than the full divinity of the Father.
But it does imply that the Divine Being in its fulness was present
in Jesus in what the early theological tradition called a distinct

mode of being.[4] Consequently the mainstream tradition felt that these modes of being – God as ultimate Source of all and God as incarnate in Jesus (and, later, a third mode of being, God as Spirit of the Body of Christ, the Church) – must correspond to some self-differentiation within the Divine Being itself. Just as I experience differentiation within my own self as I fashion relationships with others. And for the elements of this inner-divine self-differentiation traditional theology used the term 'person'.

The problem, then, was this. People then as now, theologically sophisticated and unsophisticated alike, used the language of three divine persons in one God in such a way as to suggest that these are persons much as each individual human being is a person. Then, inevitably, the impression was conveyed on which some comment has already been passed: that one of these persons, so understood, took a human nature. And the impression was further conveyed and received that the 'one person and hypostasis', in which Chalcedon found the unity of Christ, was in fact this divine person who had existed from eternity as the 'Second Person of the Blessed Trinity'. Saying such things, and understanding person in this common manner, these implications emerged which we have noticed already: a diminished sense of the humanity of Jesus living out a fully human life, or a sense of duality within Jesus between an impassible divine person and a vulnerable human nature, and sometimes both.

The mainstream theological tradition tried to combat the emergence of such misleading impressions in a number of ways. Augustine in Book Seven of his magisterial work on *The Trinity* effectively divested the word person of all ordinary meaning, leaving it to convey some sense of a distinction in divinity and no more. Others preferred the Greek term 'hypostasis', and insisted just as strongly that it had nothing in common with 'person' as normally used and understood, that nothing more or less was being said than that the Divine Being or 'substance' existed in three distinct modes of being. These modes of being were somehow perceptible in the course of creation and redemption, and they correspond, one might believe, to some mysterious self-differentiation within the Divine Being itself.

Even when the mainstream theological tradition did conclude – for Chalcedon did not specifically decide this – that the 'one person and hypostasis' in which the specific character of divine and human 'nature' is united was in fact the divine person, it was still careful to point out that here, too, the word 'person' was to be taken in an altogether unusual sense, and that it did not mean anything like what the word 'person' normally means. So, for example, when it was said that the 'one person and hypostasis' was a divine 'person and hypostasis', and that Jesus' human nature was consequently 'anhypostatic', that is to say, Jesus' human nature did not have its own 'person and hypostasis' – none of this could be taken to imply that Jesus was not a human person as we normally understand that word. For we normally take the word 'person' to mean a centre of consciousness facing at its depth the darkness of impending death, an ego, a human will burdened with its finite freedom, a mind groping amongst the uncertainties of history for some ground of hope. All of this the theological tradition would want to affirm of Jesus, and some of this was explicitly defined by conciliar decree. So Jesus was a human person in the same sense as we are human persons – except that he did not sin as we do. So to say that this human being, Jesus of Nazareth, had a divine rather than a human 'person and hypostasis' is to use these twin terms in their refined theological sense where they refer to a particular but subsistent mode of existence; it is to say that the human person of Jesus of Nazareth lived the distinctive mode of existence of God incarnate, and in doing so lived a thoroughly human life. Turning the matter around, it is to say that in a distinct mode of its existence the Divine Being lived the life of the human person, Jesus of Nazareth.

Those who understand in their proper refinements the Chalcedonian Christology, and the Trinitarian theology which in part lies behind it, will not, I think, conclude that Chalcedon said anything more, or anything different from what was said in Scripture when Jesus was said to be God's Word incarnate and 'Word' is taken to mean, as Chapter 3 expresses it in reference to the cognate term Wisdom, God himself or herself, in his or her availability to creatures, revelation to creatures, presence with or in creatures. God's word, wisdom, spirit, as Chapter 3 put it, is to be understood as God in God's own outreach to creatures. Dogma simply unpacks this insight and translates it into its own jargon, that to God's original mode of being is 'added' a distinct mode of being in individual human flesh (and perhaps yet a 'third' distinct mode of being as the spirit of a vast community moving through history). But it is always one and the same Divine Substance, the same Divine Being who is present in each mode of being, never another or a lesser one. Or, as the exegete would say, God's word or spirit is God in outreach to, God present in creatures. And the Christian claim is that this presence in its fulness is encountered in Jesus of Nazareth.

There is then no superiority of dogma in the sense that it should be taken to say something more or other than what the Scriptures say about Jesus of Nazareth – although, of course, those who speak less wisely this abstruse theological jargon, and take the word 'person', despite all professional cautions, in too usual a sense, can indeed find themselves talking about a divine person who seems to have either deprived Jesus of his human personhood, or lived with the human being in uneasy duality. Then indeed a bowdlerized Chalcedon says something more and different from what the Scriptures say, and Karl Barth has to issue his stern warning that the Scriptures give us no licence at all to talk about a discarnate Word, a Word described as person or subject before or beyond the person of Jesus of Nazareth.

There is also, then, no 'essential' claim to superiority for Jesus when the theological tradition leading up to Chalcedon is understood according to its own systematically built-in cautions. Jesus is no more superior to other incarnations of divinity 'by definition' as a result of Chalcedon, than he is or was as a result of the earlier Christologies of Scripture. An inspiration Christology, as Hick calls the 'spirit' Christologies of New Testament times, is as fully an incarnation Christology as any other. And if such an incarnation Christology does not yield unique superiority 'by definition', neither will the others. Yet claims to unique superiority did obviously emerge, and they are sustained, even in the face of incarnational theologies in other religions. Since there appears to be no scriptural necessity to affirm that the presence of the 'full' Divine Being – for God's wisdom, word, spirit, and so on, *is God himself or herself* present to or with or in creatures – can occur only once; and there appears to be no logical necessity to affirm that the presence of the Divine Being itself in or as a human being can occur in only one human being – other religions claim such an incarnation, and fail to see any incongruity in claiming many of them – what is the ground for such claims to unique superiority? How are such claims to be assessed?

2   THE CONCEPT OF DIVINE REVELATION

If one were to consider more attentively some actual claims to unique superiority which in the course of history have in fact been made by a number of religions, one would soon see that they did not derive *by definition* from any of the usual ways of talking about the presence of the Divine Being in the world at particular times or places: presence in word, wisdom, spirit, the Word of God incarnate in Jesus according to the Fourth Evangelist, the Word of God ensouled (*empsuchos*) in Moses according to Philo. On the contrary, a claim to superiority seems always to be made at the point at which a religious vision begins to take formal shape as a structured religion against the existing structures of other, nearby religions; and the claim seems to be designed to secure members of the new religion against the comparable claims of the others, or even to win over members of the other religions. The claims to unique superiority were then, of course, expressed in terms of one or more of the usual forms for describing the presence in this world of the Divine Being itself – but they did not derive by definition from any of these. Nor indeed could they do so. There is no such thing, in that sense, as a definitive claim, or indeed as a definitive religion.

It might be well to pause at this point, to remark upon the fact – for it very much appears to be the fact – that some individuals who are now counted amongst the founders of religions, did not set out to found 'new' religions at all, and some of them may have died without having done so. The Buddha Gautama insisted that he was simply rediscovering an ancient way to an ancient city; Guru Nanak, far from wishing from the outset to add a new Sikh religion to the existing and warring religions of Hinduism and Islam, wanted more than anything else to bring about a state in which there would be 'neither Hindu nor Musulman'; and Jesus of Nazareth, to the best of our knowledge, lived and died a Jew and never even imagined the replacement of his Jewish faith with anything else. The implications of this fact may concern us shortly. They have something to say about the process by which a vision of renewal becomes domesticated in those formulated institutions, creeds, codes, and rituals which make up the structures of a religion. But for the moment it is necessary to concentrate only on the point that religions do make claims to superiority over other religions, and express these in the usual formulae for confessing divine presence in history. This point is illustrated by much of the material at the end of Chapter 3. But the dialogue is best advanced by a systematic analysis of contemporary forms of such rival claims, and of the logic within or behind them.

The Baha'i faith is perhaps the most recent to be able to claim, with good reason, the status of a world religion. Founded in the mid-nineteenth century, its principal aim is to inaugurate the new era of peace and unity for the race which, it is convinced, religion has sought from the beginning and which it contends religion alone is capable of bringing about in the end. Hence the first article of faith for the Baha'i confesses that all religions have the same 'core', all are in essence the same in their shared belief in one and the same God who works patiently through them all, out of love, for the peace and unity of the race and for the final return of all souls to himself. Few religions have so prominently proclaimed that the light which they bring is indeed the light which has enlightened, and continues to enlighten, everyone who is born into this world. Seldom does the inclusivist note strike so early and so surely in the orchestrated presentation of a faith that is to be proclaimed to the ends of the earth.

The second article of the Baha'i faith is designed to take account of the many religions which, before the Baha'ullah, succeeded each other in the course of human history. God pursued his single purpose by respecting, rather than ignoring, the ages of man. Successive divine revelations brought to successive ages a series of 'laws', each adapted to the age for which it was revealed, and all in sequence preparing for the final revelation for this age which is entrusted to the Baha'is. Hence other religions constitute a divinely revealed *praeparatio evangelica*, a preparation for the good news for this age. Correspondingly, the Baha'ullah is described in an introduction to their *Most Holy Book* as 'the One who was destined to establish the Kingdom of God on earth', and the *Most Holy Book* which came from his pen, not only reveals the new 'law' on which the future world order must rest, but names the authoritative interpreter of this 'law' and the institution which will secure the integrity of the 'law' and its interpretations. Consistent with its own logic, the Baha'i faith does not rule out yet another revelation in the future. In fact it frequently contents itself with the declaration that the present revelation is to govern the next thousand years, although it calls down the most severe divine sanctions on any who would within that period claim a divine revelation different from its own.

This very brief account of Baha'i claims is not introduced in order to enter into a debate about their substance or their possible supports. The claims are introduced rather because in form, if not in all the details of their substance, they convey a very strong sense of *déjà vu*. To put the matter bluntly, what Baha'is here do to Muslims, Christians and Jews (and other religions, presumably, despite the fact that the founder had Islam mainly in mind), is just what Muslims had done before them to Christians and Jews, and what Christians before *them* had done to Jews. There were differences in detail, of course, in the ways in which each in turn described the origins and temporary legitimacy of the ones that had gone before, but each in turn is strikingly similar to the others in two respects: in its insistence that the Divine Being did truly reveal the others and was therefore encountered in them, and in its equal insistence upon the fact that such revelations were now superseded by a (more) final or definitive one. It is perfectly clear from this group of religions at least, that claims to unique superiority are made and that they are based on theories of (successive) divine revelation. It is an understanding of divine revelation, then, that is the proffered ground of such claims, and not any logical entailment from ways of expressing the presence of the Divine Being.[5]

Now everything depends at this point on how one understands divine revelation, on how one thinks it has taken place, and what 'deposits' it has left behind. Clearly the presumption conveyed by the very similar claims made by members of the group of religions mentioned above, is: (1) revelation is to be taken as an actual unveiling, something once hidden from view is no longer hidden; (2) that the 'something' is progressively fuller or purer, so that what went before is correspondingly incomplete or unrefined. On such a presumption depend the claims to unique superiority which are common to this group. And on the further presumption that the favoured act of such divine revelation is, up to this point in time at any rate, *final*, depend further claims that, for example, a particular extant set of Scriptures is normative for believers.

Since such presumptions lie so clearly behind claims to unique superiority, two surprises await those who, keeping them firmly in mind, analyse more closely the revelatory claims which are actually made. First, such analysts would discover that different religions in this group think differently of divine revelation and its 'deposits' in history. Muslims and Baha'is, to simplify matters (but not, one may hope, excessively), think of the final revelation in terms of 'laws' deposited now in writings or books as a result of God's direct and detailed instructions to prophets – and 'prophet' means literally one who 'speaks for' another. Christians and Jews, on the other hand, are not so clear about the matter. Some of them do see in their sacred books what one would expect to find in them if God had actually dictated their contents. But others locate the act of divine revelation in events prior to the composition of Scriptures and see the latter as records, 'inspired' records no doubt, interpretations perhaps, but nonetheless records of those prior revelatory events.

Second, and consequently, our analysts would discover that Christians in the long history of their theology had devoted surprisingly little time or effort to an attempt to say what kind of event a divine act of revelation was or could be. Claims to the effect that the uniquely superior act of divine revelation had taken place are all too frequent in the long history of Christian theology; analysis of the alleged act are, until recent decades, patchy and very, very infrequent. This brief chapter would find itself greatly overburdened by even a brief review of the sudden onrush of Christian theologies of revelation which invaded our ivory towers during the 1960s and '70s. Suffice it to say that this theology moved all the way from propositional theories of revelation to theories of revelation as history.[6] And insofar as it can be considered to have reached a conclusion rather than to have petered out, this new theology looked for divine revelation to events in the histories of people or of individuals which were quite similar in kind to those suffered or enjoyed by others. The Israelites were not the only people to have escaped from serfdom, and Jesus of Nazareth was far from being the only Jew to have been put to death by the Gentiles. Jesus of Nazareth, of course, was raised from the dead – not the only one, again, for whom such claims were made – but the historical status of that 'event' is problematic, to say the least. It is an event which takes one outside history rather than occurs within history. The witness to it, consequently, bears some resemblance to witness to visions. It is perhaps not surprising that so many modern theologians describe the experience of the risen Lord by the earliest witnesses as itself a faith experience; and that suggests the main difference between the propositional view of revelation and the view of revelation as history.

On the propositional view the divine act of revelation, however it is to be imagined, resulted directly in propositions, sentences, doctrines in short. On the other view divine revelation refers to historical experiences through which people lived and to which they were somehow enabled to respond with religious faith — that faith, of course, taking specific shape, or changing, or growing in the process; and then in time they put their faith into words and, as they did so, they inevitably interpreted as acts of God the events which had so shaped their lives and the experiences through which they had come. The 'somehow' in that last sentence refers, of course, to that which enables some people to react to, say, an invasion of their country with all its mindless destruction of all they ever held dear, not with anger and despair, but with a belief in a providence that shapes our ends, however cruelly it may seem to have to do so at times. And the ambivalence of events hinted in *that* last sentence accounts for the difference in the use and understanding of the term 'revelation' from the propositional view. Some looking on the crucified Jew saw a man getting his just deserts for threatening such peace and security as his occupied country could expect to enjoy; others saw a miscarriage of justice and reflected ruefully perhaps that it was not the first and probably would not be the last; others, a Roman soldier according to one evangelist, saw in the dying Jew there and then the Son of God. That which enabled some to respond in religious faith to historical events to which others respond with anger, applause, mild interest or mere boredom, will eventually be named the Spirit of God, God as Spirit, God immanent in the persons responding as God was immanent in the key persons or events to which they were enabled to respond in this way. Revelation will then come to be understood more in inspirational terms, and the correspondence with the Christology of the first section of this chapter will not be lost on the attentive reader.

For the main difference between the propositional view of revelation and the view of revelation as history is that in the former revelation could be taken rather literally. Something – law or doctrine – was truly unveiled from or by God which was previously hidden, and since it has to be taken as quite literally God's will manifest, it naturally supersedes whatever went before, even if what went before is also allowed to have been revealed by God; and it is naturally normative for the future in such a way as to support a claim for unique superiority, and an automatic claim for the supremely normative status of the Scriptures in which it is written down. Revelation is the key concept here, faith the derivative.

In the view of revelation as history, however, the key concept is faith, religious faith which, it is believed, is enabled or 'inspired' by God. 'It is believed', one has to write, for on this view one can never escape from faith, or be rescued from its comprehensive hold on all of human life by some different kind of certainty. One lives by faith indeed, and by faith alone. The historical events are in themselves – if one can ever catch them by themselves – ambivalent. And so the concept of revelation on this view of it takes a very much second place. To put the case too simply, one does not believe because something one knows has been literally revealed; one first believes in the presence of God in some key events and persons (thus designated as key events or persons), and revelation language is then used to make one's claim that this faith, this hope, is true or will prove to be true in the end.

In the understanding of revelation language, then, to which the modern theology of revelation has inexorably moved, to speak of God being revealed in a person or an event, or in the

events that make up a person's life, is a way of making the claim
of faith that the Diving Being was thus present. It is not a way
of supplying that claim with incontrovertible ground. Indeed on
this understanding of revelation language, and on this understanding alone, the rather paradoxical statement so frequently
and rather pompously pronounced actually makes some sense:
that God remains concealed in the very act of divine revelation.
(This in turn corresponds to the christological statement that
the Divine Being is present in another 'mode of being'.) On this
understanding of it, 'revelation' does indeed translate its Greek
New Testament original *apokalypsis* (apocalypse), because it
expresses a claim of faith and hope in the present which can but
point to presence face-to-face at some definitive point in the
future: the revelation fully and properly so-called will be at the
end. It remains possible, then, for others who see the same
person and events, or who indeed participate with the former in
the latter, to conclude that no Divine Being was present, or even
that instead a demonic spirit was operative (that it is by Beel-
zebub that he does what he does). Whether this conclusion
reached by these others is to be attributed to their own obtuse-
ness or to a dearth of divine inspiration, or to other more
complicated factors, need not concern us here. What does concern us is what might be called the primacy of faith – faith by
divine Spirit moving in us allows us to detect the presence of
God in the world's history and in particular persons and events;
and hence allows us to claim that God is revealed in such persons
and events, although, paradoxically, not yet revealed 'in himself'. This leads us back by yet another route to the thoughts on
faith which concluded Chapter 2, and in particular to the
thought that people can indeed recognize each other's forms of
faith across all kinds of confessional, cultural and temporal
chasms. The merging and emerging of horizons is still intact.
But what now becomes of claims to unique superiority, and
what becomes of claims concerning the supremely normative
nature of sacred Scriptures? Both of these claims surely need for
their support a theology of revelation which, if not strictly of the
propositional kind, at least retains the primacy of revelation
over faith, as a consequence of feeling able to point to acts of
divine revelation which are manifestly such or can be proved
beyond reasonable doubt to be such?

It is difficult to supply in a short space all the ingredients for a full answer to these large questions. We should have to recall some of the conclusions of Chapter 3: that exclusivist-sounding sentences in Scripture can be seen as ways in which early Christians countered Jewish exclusivism; that they may be seen as ways of focusing the readers' minds on the full challenge of Jesus' claim upon them. But that still leaves the clause at the end of Chapter 3 about bringing all to the test of Christ. Is this or is it not the Christian claim to unique superiority in what is hoped is a slightly more palatable form? I cannot answer for the sacred author, or even for the exegete here, but from the viewpoint of the material of this chapter I can offer some suggestions.

First, the experience of bringing some religious conviction or practice to the test of Christ is altogether different from the attempt to argue the superiority of one religion over another. In the former experience one may find – one almost certainly will find – that the test of Christ proves as disruptive of one's own settled ways in the Christian churches as it proves critical of whatever other religion one may encounter. In the latter one may well miss *both* the critical exposure to the founder of Christianity *and* the critical exposure to the founder or foundational vision of another religion. For religions do have a habit of declining from the pinnacles which their founders reached, and all find ways of accommodating the original vision to what the common mass of mortals finds manageable.

Second, Christians ought to be among the first to understand that religions are not primarily theories at all (sets of doctrines to be 'proved', established and explained), but 'ways', that is to say, ways of living. For Christians profess to believe that God who is Spirit lived in Jesus of Nazareth, and was therefore revealed in the life he lived and the death in which that life was consummated. Their faith cannot be satisfied with telling the story of that life, however persuasively and with however high a degree of assent; much less can it be satisfied with distilling doctrines from that story, however accurately and with however impressive a degree of authority. These things they must do, of course, but only as an aid to the one thing necessary: to live the life, to aim at least at being able to say with Paul, 'I live now, not I, but Christ lives in me'. The relative superiority or inferiority of religions will be decided, if it ever is, by their 'ways', by the ways in which they behave, especially towards each other, and in this kind of contest theoretical claims to unique superiority are likely to lose points rather than gain them, because of the prejudice and divisiveness which such claims foster and the hostile attitudes they endorse.

Christians have no option but to search for the spirit of Jesus, since they believe it to be the divine Spirit. They suspect at least that it is characterized by a very distinctive kind of loving, by a conviction of unconditioned grace and gracefulness to all. They seek it amongst fellow-Christians, of course, but since they believe it to be the divine spirit moving through the world, and they know that God cannot be confined to churches, they will not show surprise if they sometimes recognize it in people of other religions, or of none. An essential element in the recognition-process is the quest of Jesus of Nazareth in whose life, death and resurrection, Christians believe this spirit was 'incarnate'. The records which are the *sine qua non* of this quest are the documents which the earliest followers of Jesus preserved and to which they gave a position of unique authority, because in them they recognized the person and the spirit of Jesus of Nazareth. These documents, the New Testament as they have come to be called, retain their uniquely normative position to this day, and there is little or no likelihood that they can ever be replaced. It is out of reverence for the real authority of these texts that one attempts the kind of exercise which this book, and this whole series exemplifies: to bring the cultural horizons of this age as consciously as possible into contact with the cultural horizons of the biblical documents, so that in the ensuing merging of horizons the distinctiveness of each might emerge and the normativeness of the Bible might have its real and genuine effect upon the Christian mind of the contemporary era.

NOTES

1   The paper which John Hick presented to the seminar is now published as 'An Inspiration Christology for a Religiously Plural World' in Stephen T. Davis, ed., *Encountering Jesus* (Atlanta, John Knox Press, 1987).

2   See John Hick, *God Has Many Names* (Philadelphia, Westminster Press, 1983); *Problems of Religious Pluralism* (London, Macmillan, 1985).

3 The book which most stoutly defends the right of Spirit Christologies, although it unnecessarily (in my view) denigrates Logos Christologies is G. Lampe's *God as Spirit* (Oxford, Clarendon Press, 1977).

4 Much the same point can be put in terms of the divine` kenosis` or self-emptying. This cannot be taken to mean that God shed some of the Divine Being – some divine attributes perhaps – but rather that the presence of Divine Being in a human mode of being was itself, as Cyril of Alexandria said, a condescension as it involved another mode of divine being.

5 There may well be other ways in which in other groups of religions claims to unique superiority can be made. Indeed some of the most advanced inclusivist claims, to the effect, for example, that *all* other religions are but differently structured forms of religion, as one's own tradition understands the matter, may turn out to be quite paradoxically no more than further versions of claims to unique superiority. But the group considered above does contain Christianity, and Christian claims to unique superiority are therefore best considered in terms which are common to members of that group, in terms, that is to say, of claims about divine revelations.

6 This was the title of a key collection of essays edited by Wolfhart Pannenberg, *Revelation as History* (New York, Macmillan, 1968); see also R. Latourelle, *Theology of Revelation* (New York, Alba House, 1966); H. R. Schlette, *Epiphany as History* (New York, Herder & Herder, 1969); Gabriel Moran, *The Present Revelation* (New York, Herder & Herder, 1972).

Another Test Case: Church Ministry
(1) A View from Systematic Theology

In the previous pair of chapters we began with the Scriptures. The New Testament scholar sought to discover the scriptural horizons of Christology and to set in relief some of the ways in which these might be related to later horizons of doctrinal development. The systematician then attempted to place traditional Christology in its contemporary setting, thus to raise explicitly the kind of questions which could allow the Scriptures to make their own distinctive contribution once more. In this next pair of chapters the process is reversed. First, a systematic view of church ministry will be analysed in its contemporary setting; although the setting now will be the Christian ecumenical scene rather than the worldwide inter-faith encounter. Then the New Testament scholar will look to the normative texts in order to see what shapes of ministry did then emerge and how these findings might suggest a way out of the impasse which seems to have been reached in discussions concerning ministry between the Christian Churches.

The example of a view of church ministry to be taken here is the Roman Catholic view as expressed in the course of the Second Vatican Council. The reasons for this choice are as follows: first, Roman Catholicism in this century has presented Christians with a rare incident of a general council and hence with a view of ministry, amongst many other matters of course, which can claim the highest degree of authority, at least in the Roman Church; second, although some other Churches share much of the view of ministry, as episcopal and hierarchical, which characterizes Roman Catholicism, it is the Roman Catholic view which has posed, and continues to pose, the most insuperable obstacles to ecumenism.

The Dogmatic Constitution on the Church (*Lumen Gentium*) from the Second Vatican Council (1962-4) was not the first document to be completed by the Council, yet it rightly stands at the beginning of the collection of such authoritative documents, *The Documents of Vatican II*,[1] for it is the key document for Roman Catholicism's most official understanding of itself to this point in time. Already in this document there is reference to the whole people of God as 'a holy priesthood'; the idea of the priesthood of all believers, so dear to the more progressive theologians of the Roman Church, is thereby endorsed. Yet Luther, to whom this idea was also dear, is far from being received back into the fold! For the document immediately distinguishes from this common priesthood of the faithful a 'ministerial or hierarchical priesthood', and it states quite explicitly that these 'differ from one another in essence and not only in degree' (*Lumen Gentium*, n10). The ministerial priest, the document continues, enjoys a 'sacred power', by which he brings about the eucharistic sacrifice, and rules the priestly people. A little later it is said that 'those ministers who are endowed with sacred power are servants of their brethren' (n18); so if we want to understand a rule which is nonetheless a service we must obviously know what kind of power is here in question and how some, and not others, acquire it.

The first thing that must be said about this sacred power is that it is what makes a priest a priest. So much can be gathered from what has already been said about difference in kind between hierarchical priesthood and common priesthood of the faithful. But what kind of priesthood is here? Priesthood very like the Jewish priesthood, must be the answer; for twice, in the Vatican II document on Bishops (n15) and in the document on Priests (n3), Hebrews 5.1 is implicitly quoted, as it is said that bishops and priests are 'taken from among men and appointed for men in the things which pertain to God, in order to offer gifts and sacrifices for sins'. The phrase about their being taken from among men reinforces the impression that their priesthood is different in kind from that of other Christians; and the similarity with Jewish priesthood is further reinforced by the insistence that they have a sacrifice to offer which only they can offer. The sacrifice they have to offer is the sacrifice of Jesus the Christ who offered himself 'once and for all' to his Father, and if it sounds paradoxical that a sacrifice once offered 'once and for all' (Constitution on the Church, n28) should be regularly offered thereafter, it can only be said that it is thereafter 're-presented' or 'applied' (see BEM, *Euch.* n8 com.). In any case the Eucharist – for that is what is here in question – is considered to be a sacrifice, and only the priests are enabled to offer it. And the power which enables them, and them alone, to do so, is the power that gives them a priesthood different in essence from any other.

The quest for a clear concept of the nature and distribution of this special and sacred priestly power is complicated by a number of factors with which in the documents of Vatican II it is connected. First, as the power of orders (*potestas ordinis*), it is often said to be combined in the same persons with the power of jurisdiction (*potestas jurisdictionis*), and with the power to teach with authority (*potestas magisterii*). Sometimes the doc-uments give the impression that the first of these powers is primary and source of all others, and this would seem sensible in a way, because the Church is in the business of mediating God's grace for the salvation of humankind. Therefore, it might be expected, only those who could claim some special role in the mediation could also claim a comparable role in teaching what is to be believed about it and in acting as officers of good order in the resulting community. That is the impression conveyed by the following statement: 'Episcopal consecration, together with the office of sanctifying, also confers the offices of teaching and of governing' (Constitution on the Church, n21).

Yet the powers of teaching and governing are not altogether aligned with the 'sacred power' of priesthood. For one thing, the Bishop of Rome exercises a power of teaching and juris-diction quite beyond that of the other bishops – they can exercise supreme power over the whole Church only together and in union with him; he can exercise supreme power in his own right. Yet he appears to have no higher power of priesthood, and one has to wonder whether there were two original conferrings? For another, the power of jurisdiction (or governing) in part-icular has led to an acquisition over the centuries of titles con-nected with such power, which clearly owe their origins to the most secular of institutions; some poor misguided churchmen still go about today expecting people to address them as 'My

Lord', and 'Your Grace', and other titles of secular origin from feudal or imperial ages now long past; and it is difficult, to say the least, to see how such titles, or the kind of power they once connoted, can be associated with Christian ministry.

Secondly, this sacred power which results in priesthood confers priesthood, apparently, in different degrees. Bishops, according to Vatican II, receive the 'fulness of the sacrament of orders', or 'the high priesthood'; those who are called simply priests, on the other hand, 'do not possess the highest degree of the priesthood' and are dependent on bishops in the exercise of their power. (Constitution on the Church, nn21,28). In the words of the Council's Decree on Priests, the ministerial role enjoyed fully by bishops 'has been handed down to priests in a limited degree' (n2).

Now it is naturally not easy to understand what these higher and lower, or limited degrees of the 'sacred power' can mean to priesthood. It is obvious enough in the case of the power of jurisdiction, and even in the case of the power of authoritative teaching, that one man's power to impose a ruling may be limited by the higher power of another man, and one man's authority to teach limited by the higher authority of another man (women, of course, are not allowed to exercise any of these powers in the Roman Catholic Church). But it is not at all clear how one man can be a priest in a higher or more limited degree than another. If the 'sacred power' of priests is, as the documents of Vatican II on more than one occasion describe it, that which enables them 'to offer sacrifice and to remit sins' (Decree on Priests, n2), what could possibly be the effect of its presence in higher or more limited degrees? Sacrifice more or less fully offered, sins not always remitted to the same degree?

It is easy enough to understand how such theories of degrees came about. In the exercise of functions which they had gradually monopolized, bishops of the early Church wished to have helpers but still retain their own power. The most obvious way to do this is to have the helpers participate in power, but to a lesser degree. The Decree on Priests (n2) is careful not to say that this process of appointing priests with a limited degree of priesthood (something significantly less than 'the highest degree of priesthood') was handed down by the apostles of Jesus, much less by Jesus himself. Thus the possibility of church origin for this process is tacitly allowed, and with it the suspicion that the ensuing impression of degrees in the sacred power of priesthood simply follows from the more easily under-stood degrees in the other powers, namely, the power of juris-diction and the power to teach with authority. But, of course, to the extent that we are then given the impression of one undifferentiated sacred power – simultaneously enabling people to sacrifice, govern and teach – occurring in different degrees at different levels of a hierarchy, to that extent we raise again the issue of the apparent non-alignment of these powers. The questions become more rather than less acute: what is this 'sacred power' so frequently claimed in these documents? When and by whom was it conferred? Why do some have it, and not others?

It might be wise to consider some efforts to deduce from assumed axioms the answers to this interconnected set of ques-tions, before going on to analyse the scattered evidence in the Documents of Vatican II on which answers might be based. Someone might say, for example, that a sacrifice by definition requires a priest in order that it be offered, that is to say, in order that it *be*. But such a statement is either tautologous and harm-less – a priest is one who offers a sacrifice so that anyone who offers anything sacrificially is thereby a priest – or it lays upon the person who makes it the obligation of showing what kind of power is necessary, and why, and whence it comes, in order that some should be able to offer sacrifice and others not be able to do so; and we are back again to our original questions. This might seem too obvious for words, but it seems necessary never-theless to say it, if only to prove that the dispute between Protestants and Catholics as to whether the Eucharist is or is not to be called a sacrifice will not of itself, no matter how it is resolved, settle the question as to whether or not priests with special powers are needed, or indeed tolerable in Christian Chur-ches. There is no difficulty at all in conceiving of the Eucharist as a sacrifice and yet concluding that it needs no priests different 'in essence' from the rest of those who join in the offering; or, to put the same point in another way, concluding that all who join in the offering are thereby priests, and the common priesthood of the faithful is therefore quite adequate to the occasion.

The point might be pressed, of course, and this kind of answer considered unsatisfactory, in the following way. It might be granted that in general sacrifices do not need priests especially empowered (or that whoever in fact offers a sacrifice is by that fact a priest), but in the special case of the Eucharist, since the victim is the risen Lord Jesus, he needs to be made present in order that the sacrifice be offered, and that act of bringing about his 'real presence', as it is called, requires a special power, and especially empowered priests. Here is the need for a special 'sacred power' which makes the priests who possess it different 'in essence' from other priests more generally so-called. What can be said to such a case? First, that, since it centres now upon the 'real presence', its validity or invalidity is independent of the issue of whether and in what sense the Eucharist can be called a sacrifice. Second, that it simply raises the questions once again, and all the more acutely the more cogent it is thought to be: *what* power (to make Jesus really present), when and by whom conferred, and why on some and not on others? So, to the evidence of the Documents of Vatican II.

These documents come nearest to identifying the source and nature of the 'sacred power' which they mention so frequently, when they point to an outpouring of the Holy Spirit; and they come closest to answering the question as to why some have this sacred power and others do not have it, when they point in particular to 'a *special* outpouring of the Holy Spirit' (Constitution on the Church, n21) coming upon and/or creating a special group of people, presumably. The 'sacred power' then is the Holy Spirit, but 'poured out' and received in a 'special' way by some Christians as distinct from others. For all Christians receive the Holy Spirit at baptism, of course, and when confirmation became a distinct ritual, at confirmation also, and this reception of the Holy Spirit is the basis of Christian ministry in general, or of what is called in particular the common priesthood of the faithful. Indeed the general reception of the Holy Spirit is thought to supply the source and identity of what are called the 'charisms', those spiritual gifts of teaching, prophecy, healing, and so on, which different people possess and all of which co-operate towards the building up of the Christian community in the world. But we are meant to take it, apparently, that a special outpouring and reception of the Spirit makes some

men priests in a manner different in essence from the manner in
which the generality of Christians are made ministers of grace
and of diverse graces to each other and to humankind. (It is
difficult to find in the documents any reference which would
answer the further question: What or when is the 'especially
special' outpouring that would have conferred higher or lower
degrees of the same sacred power on different groups within this
special group of priests? – but then, it has been remarked already, it is difficult to understand what could possibly be meant
by degrees of priesthood in any case).

Now it is, of course, for the scripture scholar to say how much
real evidence there is for an outpouring of the Spirit so 'special'
that it can be believed both to have taken place and to have
equipped a special group of Jesus' followers with a sacred power
of priesthood different in essence from all other priesthood –
although even the humble systematician can notice that of the
scriptural texts appealed to in the above quotation from the
Constitution on the Church (n21), Acts 1.8 and 2.4 refer to
power and an outpouring of Spirit for, apparently, apostles,
whereas John 20.22–3 has no such restricted group in view, and
refers to the recipients merely as 'the disciples'. But be that as
it may – and we shall hear from the exegete shortly – the systematician who is aware, as he or she ought to be, of the main
movements in the development of doctrine, can and must make
the following observations upon this view put forward during
Vatican II about the Holy Spirit and sacred power and priesthood different in essence from all other priesthood.

The Constitution on the Church (again in n21, for example)
mentions 'consecration' as the action at or by which those called
to the high priesthood receive the special sacred power. The
term 'consecration' refers to that which earlier, in the latter half
of the second century, came to be called ordination, and that
term in turn was an adaptation, certainly in the Roman province
of Africa, of the term (ordinare) for the actual appointment to
imperial service. In short, as with many of the terms and structures then coming into use in an increasingly organized and
spreading Christian community, there was a great deal of such
adaptation from civic structures of the time. In the Traditio
Apostolica of Hippolytus, which dates from the first half of the
third Christian century, the ordination of the bishop involves,

amongst other things, the calling down upon the candidate of 'the power of high-priestly charisma of the Spirit'. So it would seem that, at that point of time at least, the hierarchical system envisaged by Vatican II is already in place.

Two things need to be noted, however: both equally crucial to the present context. The first has to do with the first two Christian centuries or, to put the matter in another way, with the century closest to the earliest origins of the Christian community. In that time there is no evidence whatever to suggest that any special charism of the Spirit was needed in order to empower any particular person or class of people to 'bring about' the real presence of the risen Lord in the Eucharist. There is in short, no sign at all of a priesthood which could be deemed different 'in essence' from a common priesthood of the faithful. Leadership structures are, of course, continuing to emerge and to develop and there is undoubtedly much correlation between leadership of the community and presidency of the community's most essential sacramental rite, the Eucharist. But the charisms that are needed for leadership in its various forms, as these are identified, are charisms for just that. The Spirit equips the community with men and women gifted to meet its many and varied needs. But there is no special charism needed for any particular person in order to 'bring about' the Eucharist; and the charism needed for presidency of the eucharistic celebration, if one is needed, is not in the least additional to some other charism already possessed, e.g. that of prophet.

That same point can be put in a slightly different manner by reflecting on the development of Eucharist and its theology. The real presence of Jesus in the Eucharist was not originally 'timed' for the 'moment of consecration' as it much later came to be called, the moment, that is to say, at which the president pronounced the words, 'This is my body', 'This is my blood', over bread and wine. (Indeed there is one piece of firm evidence of a eucharistic prayer which did not have any 'words of consecration' at all – the eucharistic prayer of Addai and Mari). In fact in these same early centuries it is impossible to distinguish a real presence of Jesus in the bread and wine from a real presence of Jesus in the celebrating community of those who offer, take, bless God for, break, pour, give, and receive, all the time invoking the Spirit of God to make Jesus, the life-giving Spirit, present in their lives as they commemorate the breaking and giving of his earthly body and the shedding of his blood. Spirit Christology is very powerfully present once more in early eucharistic prayer and early eucharistic theology.[2] It is impossible to avoid the powerful impression that to this new community of Jesus-followers, God who is Spirit and who made Jesus also life-giving Spirit, is being asked (*epiclesis*) in this eucharistic re-presentation (*anamnesis*) of broken bread and shared wine, to pour that life-giving Spirit into this celebrating group so that, filled with the same Spirit as Jesus was, they become the Body of Christ, and Jesus really present in and through them in the world. The community is the real celebrant of the Eucharist, the 'priest' (if that term needs to be used), and it is in the community sharing the offered bread and wine that Jesus becomes really present as the life-giving Spirit that he was and is – *if*, of course, he does become present, for Eucharists too can fail or be distorted by the malice and stupidity of Christians. The community in this matter as in others may, of course, act through one of its leaders, a member of a group of presbyters (not priests) or a prophet, but it is nonetheless the community which celebrates and its reception of the Spirit is quite sufficient for this act; no member needs an extra special sacred power of priesthood in order to 'bring about' the Eucharist, not even if the Eucharist, as for a variety of reasons it might well be, is to be considered a sacrifice.

The second thing that needs to be noted in this context is the kind of account that can be given, and has been given, of the process by which, as Schillebeeckx put it, the rich and varied ministry of the early Christian community became 'sacerdotalized'.[3] Because this process is a long and complicated one, to insert an adequate account of it here would take us far beyond the limits laid down for this chapter, and indeed for this book. So we shall have to be satisfied with a caricature. A caricature, I hasten to add, is a very accurate portrait in its way. It merely exaggerates certain features at the expense of others for purposes of drawing particular attention to them: but the features do exist, and they are prominent. A caricature, of course, is usually

drawn with humorous intent, but, apart altogether from the fact
that some might not find this one at all funny, nothing as light-
hearted as humour is here intended.

The language of priesthood was used of the Christian community from New Testament times. This is the language which
is still used when the Documents of Vatican II refer to the
common or general priesthood of all the faithful. It is language
used, as Schillebeeckx says, allegorically. In other words, it is
not to be taken to imply that there are now priests in the
community of the new covenant who are priests in the same
sense and in the same way as priests in the original covenant –
standing between the people and God and empowered to perform cultic acts for the salvation of the people and the glory of
God which the people in general are not empowered to perform.
On the contrary, in the new covenant all have equal access to
God's grace; they need no mediators after the one who has
opened up for them this access. They are therefore their own
priests, or they are not priests at all, since in the cultic sense of
the word 'priests' they no longer need priests. They can do for
themselves what their predecessors once needed priests to do for
them; so they can be called priests by allegory. The divine
Spirit is poured out on all of them who will receive it, and they
are gifted in different ways to meet community needs, but
priesthood in the literal sense of the original covenant is no
longer one of these needs.

As leaders emerged in the nascent and spreading Christian
communities, however, the sacerdotal or priestly language came
to be applied also to them and, gradually, to their special role or
function, particularly within the eucharistic celebration, the
pivotal act of the community's very existence. For a time it was
recognized that the language of priesthood was still in this use
of it allegorical. Indeed into the fifth Christian century
'Augustine continues to refuse to call bishops and presbyters
"priests" in the real sense, in the sense of being mediators between Christ and the community.'[4] Yet there were factors at
work which would soon give this priestly language when applied
to community leaders much more than a mere allegorical sense.
These factors too are many and some more fleeting than others:
for example Cyprian in the third century calls the bishop who
presides at the Eucharist a priest and says that he stands in

Jesus' place.[5] This already goes far beyond the New Testament belief that the very least of the brethren must be for us Jesus or in Jesus' place, and it no doubt contributes to the impression that a leader really does stand between the rest of us and God. But the most persistent factor, and the one which finally brought about that distinction between leaders and laity that allows Vatican II to talk about difference in essence between their 'priesthoods', was that gradual change in the structure of leadership itself by which it continued to imitate secular structures and so came to involve a difference of 'order' (*ordo*) or estate (*status*) between clergy and laity, with a simultaneous monopoly of ministries and a consequent assimilation of other powers to the power of jurisdiction. In other words, aided by a series of historical and political changes during the decline of the Roman Empire, bishops assumed a power of jurisdiction very similar to that exercised by civic magistrates or prefects, a power which placed them above both presbyters and people, but which was shared with the presbyters rather than the people. It was gradually understood to be a power which set those who had it aside in a different 'order' from others, as it used to do in secular circles, but since it was now wielded in the Church, it was all the more naturally thought of as a 'sacred power'. It was all too easy to assume that this 'sacred power', with its intrinsically hierarchical implications, applied to 'bringing about' the Eucharist as much as it applied to governing a community and teaching. And in this way the impression came about, which is otherwise so difficult to understand, that bishops had a higher degree of the power of priesthood than had presbyters who were now simply called 'priests'.

From the vantage point of development of doctrine, then, the systematician can conclude that there is nothing original, in the sense of belonging to the original revelation which came in Jesus to his early followers, about the theology of priesthood presented in the Documents of Vatican II. But two points simply must be made before a final consideration of the effects of this theology upon our separated Christian brethren.

First, it would be plain foolishness to conclude that this briefest account of development somehow implies a leaderless Christian community, or even to conclude that it implies that Roman Catholic forms of ecclesial leadership are indefensible.

Neither could be further from the truth. The Christian community was never without leaders. Indeed, from a purely social and political point of view anarchy is inconceivable in any community which, like the Christian community, has truth to protect and a way of life to propagate. Christians believe that the Holy Spirit always has endowed and always will endow it with suitable leaders in suitable leadership structures, and these leaders and their offices must of course have their 'sacred power' in order to fulfil their functions in the community – and that 'sacred power' has its source and identity in the same Spirit. Since we know the character of the Holy Spirit from the life and death of Jesus we also know, even if he had not explicitly told us, that this sacred power cannot be exercised by lording it over others as happens with the leaders of the peoples. It must be power made perfect in what to the world looks like weakness, that is to say, in menial service to all. And, of course, it is as obvious now as it was in the days when Christians still used priestly language allegorically, that the leaders or ministers who secure as best they can the unity of the Christian people, should preside at the sacrament by which such unity is brought about, the Eucharist. What does *not* follow is that it is these leaders who, as distinct from the whole celebrating community, 'bring about' the Eucharist, who effect the real presence of Jesus, first, in the Eucharist, and then through the Eucharist in the Church, and through the Church in the world. The Holy Spirit which all receive at baptism enables all to bring about Eucharist and real presence in Church and world, and equips some with the charisms of leadership, amongst many other charisms, as the Church requires. The forms of leadership have evolved in various ways from the earliest centuries and the Roman Catholic papal and episcopal form is as legitimate as any other, provided of course that its leaders exercise their ministry in the true Spirit.

Secondly, lest there be some residual suspicion that the Roman Catholic Church, and perhaps other Churches with similar episcopal structures and similar theologies of priesthood, are being singled out for critical attention, something must be said about some of the Churches which have, apparently, eschewed hierarchy. It is not enough to say about these, as is sometimes said, and often with good reason, that they are more

'clerical' in fact than their advertised ecclesiologies would lead
one to suspect. It is necessary to add that they do all of them
have their officers of good order, as well as those officially
licensed to preach or teach; that the former have real authority
(power of jurisdiction) even if it is exercised after the manner of
modern courts rather than the courts of kings and emperors,
and that teaching too is subjected to official scrutiny, and 'heresy
trials' are possible in order to protect the truth of the Christian
gospel. Offices and officers may differ but the *potestas jurisdictionis* and the *potestas magisterii* is every bit as real.

Surely, though, the Churches which eschew hierarchy would
agree that it is the community which celebrates Eucharist and
brings about the real presence; that a properly 'ordained' leader
should, of course, preside with all the real authority or 'sacred
power' which he or she already has, but that he or she does not
have and does not need any extra priestly power or authorization
in order that Eucharist should take place? Surely, then, in
respect of this particular part of theology, the Roman Catholic
Church, and some others, are being singled out? It is not at all
certain that this is the case, and there is some reason to think
that it is not in fact the case. The ordination practices of some
of these Churches, together with a total embargo, *at least* in
practice, on any celebration of Eucharist unless a specially and
properly ordained minister can preside, could suggest that no
real belief exists that the community itself is celebrant. Instead,
some implicit theology, *at least* implicit, still clings to the need
for people with specially conferred sacred powers, and the mediators of grace, real priests for all intents and purposes, are with
us once again. It will then not matter, of course, whether these
are chosen by a congregation or provided by a bishop, for such
matters will affect provenance, not status. If some Protestant
communities, then, do finally overcome the obstacles which
they place on the path of ecumenism – the refusal, for example,
to have anything to do with a Catholic Mass because of their
views about its theology – they may still have to face, on all
fours with their Catholic brethren, the deeper challenge which
would acknowledge a communal 'concelebration' of Eucharist
by all members of a Christian people, who all share in the equal
privilege and awesome responsibility of receiving the same
Spirit and the same 'sacred power' to make Jesus really present

in the world. They may have to face the full challenge of using the word 'priest' allegorically of *all* priests, so that the full extent and the full claims of Christian community in the world may emerge from behind all present putative mediators. Can *all* break bread together in sacramental act, and so make Christ present, or can they not?

It does appear to be true, however, that in the Roman Catholic Church, and in some other episcopal Churches, much more than in Churches which reject hierarchy, dire implications for ecumenism emerge from the very manner in which jurisdictional and magisterial authority distort the understanding of the 'sacred power' which is operative in Eucharist. In short, a Church, any Church, which affords such a central place to Eucharist in the whole of Christian life and yet denies the 'sacred power' to bring about Eucharist to any but its own duly ordained ministers, or at best to duly ordained ministers of very similarly organised Churches, does a quite exceptional amount of damage to prospects for Christian unity and, consequently, does very grave damage indeed to Christian life in general. It would be well to end with an analysis of this damage that is done by allowing the structures of official leadership to restrict the presence of the eucharistic Spirit or 'sacred power' to its own confines, and of the way in which this damage might in the future be avoided.

In the Decree on Priests (n4), Vatican II had this to say about the Eucharist and its place in Christian life: 'The other sacraments, as well as every ministry of the Church and every work of the apostolate, are linked with the holy Eucharist and are directed towards it. For the most holy Eucharist contains the Church's entire spiritual wealth, that is, Christ himself, our Passover and living bread. Through his very flesh, made alive and life-giving by the Holy Spirit, he offers life to humankind. Humankind is thereby invited and led to offer itself, its labour, and all created things together with him. Hence the Eucharist shows itself to be the source and the apex of the whole work of preaching the gospel.'

Now, surely, this is true, and should be acceptable even to those Churches not noticeable for their frequent celebration of the Eucharist. For in the Eucharist the life of Jesus and its Spirit is recalled in the *anamnesis* or representation of the death in

which he consummated that life. In the breaking and taking of
bread and the sharing of the cup in the course of this beseeching
commemoration, the power of enriching and self-giving grace is
felt which can transform the whole of life, life itself takes on the
character of Jesus' Spirit, and the Christian 'way' of life forms
itself in the world, evoked and shaped also by the stumbling,
searching word of the preacher. His word at its best becomes
prophetic and at its worst does little harm. For this central and
formative experience of the Christian faith in the world, surely
it is true to say, other sacraments like baptism, and other ministries, prepare; and from it unconditioned grace to all human
beings may flow through the most practical of channels to
irrigate a near-devastated earth.

Yes, but the more truly Vatican II has perceived all of this,
the more tragically mistaken it must be thought to be in its
efforts to confine the celebration of 'valid' Eucharists to ministers of the Roman Catholic Church and to ministers of the
Eastern Orthodox Churches; the more mean and grudging must
be thought to be its allowance that yet other Churches and
'ecclesial communities' retain some of the means of grace.
Eucharist cannot be thought to mean so much, and such implications as these still be avoided. Logic takes its own toll from
the most authoritative documents, regardless of the power of
jurisdiction and the *magisterium* of those who issue them.

The same primacy of power of jurisdiction over all other
manifestations of 'sacred power' or Holy Spirit which attempts
to confine eucharistic ministry to priests different in essence
from the general priesthood of the faithful, ensures also that
official attitude of the Roman Church to ecumenism by which
that Church has never officially envisaged the success of the
ecumenical movement on any terms other than the return of all
our separated brethren to the Church of Rome. That ecumenism
is expected to result in such a return to Rome is made cuttingly
clear in Vatican II's Decree on Ecumenism. 'The result will be
that little by little, as the obstacles to perfect ecclesiastical communion are overcome, all Christians will be gathered, in a
common celebration of the Eucharist, into that unity of the one
and only Church which Christ bestowed on his Church from
the beginning.' In case anyone should wonder whether that
'unity of the one and only Church' is still to come or is here

already, the passage continues: 'This unity, we believe, dwells in the Catholic Church as something she can never lose' (n4). And in case anyone might still wish to think that the 'C' was really meant to be lower case, that some future catholic church is envisaged, but not the present Roman Catholic Church, the document corrects any such aberrant views by insisting that 'it was to the apostolic college alone, of which Peter is the head, that we believe Our Lord entrusted all the blessings of the New Covenant, in order to establish on earth the one Body of Christ into which all those should be fully incorporated who already belong in any way to God's people' (n3). It is sadly obvious then why, when the Decree allows that 'some, even very many, of the most significant elements or endowments which together go to give life to the Church herself can exist outside the visible boundaries of the Catholic Church: the written word of God; the life of grace; faith, hope and charity, along with other interior gifts of the Spirit and visible elements', it feels bound to add immediately: 'All of these, which come from Christ and lead back to him, belong by right to the one Church of Christ' (n3). And the Decree as a whole leaves one in no doubt as to which Church that is.

Yet the same Decree declares that 'if the influence of events or of the times has led to deficiencies in conduct, in church discipline, or even in the formulation of doctrine (which must be carefully distinguished from the deposit of faith), these should be appropriately rectified at the proper moment' (n6). If the analysis by the systematician in this chapter has any force or validity, then there is and has been a deficiency in the formulation of the doctrine concerning eucharistic ministry, and in particular in consequent confinement of the 'sacred power' to bring about Eucharist to those who quite legitimately monopolize other kinds of leadership authority in the Church and have the 'power' or Spirit to exercise these in a Christian fashion. Such deficiency is undoubtedly due to the influence of events and times long past, but it has today the effect of placing an enormous obstacle, not only to the progress of ecumenism, but to the development of a fuller Christian eucharistic life in the world. For if the Eucharist is prevented from bringing about (Decree on Ecumenism, n2) unity amongst fellow-Christians because some of these must first acknowledge the power of

jurisdiction and of teaching of particular prelates, then it is
unlikely, to say the least to be able to bring about the unity of
all God's children in the divided race.[6]

The systematician can only analyse a doctrine in its contemporary cultural and historical setting and suggest that the
doctrine of eucharistic ministry would be more in accord with
the 'deposit of faith' if it were acknowledged that all Christians
who receive the Spirit of Jesus are valid concelebrants of
Eucharist in the world, and that they neither need nor should wait
upon inter-church agreement concerning those forms of ecclesiastical authority which have to do with governing. The latter
also embody 'charisms' and the power of the same Spirit, but
they come in optional varieties. The damage that is done by
giving priority to these offices of good order in the Church over
the unifying dynamic of Eucharist celebrated in all Churches
and across all church boundaries by the common priesthood of
all the faithful, *is* done by allowing the 'sacred power' undoubtedly operative in these offices to monopolize and thereby
distort the 'sacred power', the presence of Spirit in the whole
Christian community that continues to attempt to bring about
Eucharist. The liberating and enriching effects of reversing
such priorities are truly incalculable; the effects of moving to an
immediate acknowledgement of the 'validity' of the Eucharists
of any Christian community that lives by Jesus' 'way' and his
truth, and of treating as truly optional the governmental structures which have evolved, and are still evolving in different
Christian communities. The systematician can bring such analysis of tradition and of contemporary consequences to the dialogue with the Scriptures, and wait to see how the scripture
scholar reacts when the Scriptures are searched with such
horizons of experience fully conscious now in the mind.

NOTES

1 The Documents of Vatican II, ed. Walter M. Abbott (London,
   Geoffrey Chapman, 1966). See also *Baptism, Eucharist and Ministry*
   [BEM] (Geneva, WCC, 1982).
2 See John H. McKenna, *Eucharist and Holy Spirit* [Alcuin Club Collections 57] (Great Wakering, Mayhew-McCrimmon, 1975).
3 Edward Schillebeeckx, *The Church with a Human Face* (London,
   SCM, 1985), pp. 144ff. This book should be required reading for all
   educated Catholics.

4 Schillebeeckx, op. cit., p. 144.
5 The belief that priests possess the sacred power of priesthood in a more
   limited degree than bishops occurs in an even more questionable form
   in those places in the Documents of Vatican II where it is said that
   priests who celebrate the Eucharist do in a certain sense make the
   bishop present to the celebrating groups. This kind of language makes
   dangerous use of the words 'make present', for it conveys now far too
   strong an impression of mediators standing in sequence between God
   and the Christian community; the priest makes the bishop present, the
   bishop, *vice* Jesus, makes Jesus really present...The hierarchical
   image can, unless care is taken, assume quite sinister proportions.
6 The argument of this chapter is fully in line with the spirit of BEM,
   which asks all churches to examine their forms of ordained ministry
   and suggests mutual recognition of ministries, pointing out how wrong
   it would be to single out one of these ministries as exclusively valid,
   and how inconsistent with Eucharist are unjustifiable confessional
   oppositions (*Min.* nn52, 55, 38, 39 com., *Euch.* n20). Furthermore, this
   chapter clearly distinguishes between ordained ministers authorized
   and graced to serve and 'centre' the Christian community, and people
   with 'special power' to make Jesus present and 'bring about Eucharist';
   there is good reason why the former should normally preside at the
   Eucharist (*Min.* n14 com.), but no need at all for the latter. This, too,
   is fully in accord with BEM, which insists quite rightly that ordination
   itself is 'an act of the whole community', albeit performed by those
   appointed and responsible for the orderly transmission of ministry
   (*Min.* nn41, 29, 37). I must, however, confess some residual unease
   with statements in BEM to the effect that ordained ministers are
   'representatives of Jesus Christ to the community', or of 'the divine
   initiative', or that they are a 'visible focus' of communion between
   Christ and members of his body (*Min.* nn11, 14; *Euch.* n29). Such
   images of human intermediaries convey a very one-sided impression,
   unless this is immediately cancelled by equally explicit statements to
   the effect that the members in their different ways are equally
   representatives of Jesus Christ and foci of communion with him for the
   ordained ministry.

6

Another Test Case: Church Ministry
(2) A View from New Testament Theology

The issue of ministry is an appropriate test case because it has a more practical edge than Christology and because it is so important in current ecumenical discussions. If Christology is at the heart of the faith of Christianity, ministry is what determines the shape and structures of Christianity. If the ecumenical movement is to progress, it must find a way to resolve or move beyond the impasse over ministry. More important, if Christianity is to be properly equipped for existence in the 'post-Christian' West and is to take realistic account of its growth and vitality elsewhere, it must be prepared to rethink its understanding of ministry from the foundation upwards. Here the dialogue of New Testament theology and of theology with the New Testament can and should play a major role.

An indication of the recognition that such a rethink is necessary is the consistent emphasis on 'the ministry of the whole people of God' in recent ecumenical statements.[1] That is to say, the recognition, many would say very belated recognition, that ministry is not the exclusive prerogative of *the* ministry = the ordained clergy. Equally indicative , however, is the fact that in most of these documents so very little is said about 'the ministry of the whole people of God'. A few opening paragraphs, and then on to the main business of the statement – viz. discussion of *the* ministry. Of course, that is simply a reflection of the disputes and divisions of Christian history. But it is nonetheless significant that there are so few controversial issues on the matter of the ministry of all Christians. There can be agreement because thought and practice has not yet moved beyond first principles. No one really knows yet what 'the ministry of the whole people of God' amounts to.

It is appropriate in a book like this, therefore, to look afresh at the foundational documents of Christianity to remind ourselves of what these foundations were. Since we are still at the level of first principles the claim of our canonical texts to have a substantial if not determinative say on what these principles are would be hard to gainsay. Here again only a few samples and a fairly basic treatment is possible, but sufficient at least to point up the issues and to sketch out something of the New Testament side of the dialogue. In response to my dialogue partner the obvious examples are priesthood and Eucharist, with ordination as an inevitable corollary.

1   PRIESTHOOD

One of the most striking features of the New Testament for student or exegete or Christian in general is its treatment of priesthood. What is so astonishing is the complete absence from its pages of a distinction between 'priest' and 'laity', of the thought that some Christians may or must needs exercise a priesthood which is not the prerogative of others. It is astonishing because it is so unusual, and was so distinctive at the time. Fundamental to the Judaism from which Jesus and Christianity emerged was the understanding that some members of the community of faith must be set apart to serve as intermediaries between God and his people. The same understanding began to re-emerge within Christianity itself quite early on, particularly with Cyprian and Hippolytus, who make ready use of the OT categories of priest and sacrifice in reference to the Eucharist. But with the New Testament writings it is different. The New Testament stands as an exceptional testimony to a different understanding of the way in which God's people may approach him, and one which marks it off both from the Old Testament and from what was subsequently to become the pattern of Catholic Christianity.[2]

Not only so, but the first Christian communities were quite distinct on this point within the sweep of the religious spectrum of the time. Priesthood and sacrifice were fundamental to all religions of the Greco-Roman world. Priest and sacrifice were established features in every town and city. It was taken for granted that friendly societies and trade guilds would be attached to some temple and look to priestly ministry for important cultic ritual. Jewish synagogues in the diaspora were an accepted peculiarity in their lack of and failure to participate in a local sacrificial cult; at the same time, however, they underlined their distinctiveness by sending the temple tax annually to support priesthood and cult in the national centre at Jerusalem. But the first Christian congregations were an oddity indeed – religious groups without priest or sacrifice.

The evidence of the New Testament is well known and can be described quite briefly.

(a) The world 'priest' is never used in the NT to describe a group of Christians to distinguish them from other Christians. Acts 6.7 reports that 'a great crowd of priests were obedient to the faith', but that particularly distinctiveness belonged to their role within Judaism and was not part of the faith which they had adopted. The only times when 'priest' or 'priesthood' is used of Christians as such are to be found in 1 Peter and Revelation. 1 Peter calls on his readers to aspire to become 'a holy priesthood', and describes them as 'a royal priesthood' (1 Pet. 2.5, 9). And Revelation twice speaks the praise of him who 'made us priests to God' (Rev. 1.6; 5.10). The point is that these descriptions refer to *all* Christians. In the thought of these writers all Christians are priests, not simply a sub-group within the ranks of Christian believers.

In the light of these texts the failure of other NT writers to allude to Christian priests as a group distinct from other Christians cannot be accidental. Evidently they did not exist. The silence of Paul at this point is eloquent. For he gives us a fuller insight into earliest Christian churches than any other NT writer. And he provides various lists of ministries which evidently were exercised in a wide range of Christian congregations (Rom. 12.6–8; 1 Cor. 12.8–10, 29; Eph. 4.11). But none of them include the ministry of priest. Even in 1 Corinthians where he has to deal with a whole series of problems, including disorder at the common meal and Lord's Supper, and where the need for leadership was self-evident, he nowhere refers his readers to a priest, or calls on anyone to act in such a capacity. So too in the Pastoral Epistles, where the concept and practice of ministry has become more developed and more structured, even there no thought of a Christian priesthood is to be found. The same is true in the other main NT writing which provides some information about the earliest churches – the Acts of the Apostles. Different ministries, including those of 'elder' and 'bishop' are envisaged (Acts. 14.23; 20.28), but never 'priest'. Evidently it never occurred to these first Christian churches and writers that a priest was necessary for the functioning of a church as church or desirable for its well-being.

The Gospels naturally do not provide much information in this area. But it may be of relevance to recall one of the points on which Matthew indicates that Christians should be distinct from their Jewish neighbours – 'you are not to be called rabbi, for you have one teacher, and you are all brethren. And call no man your father on earth, for you have one Father, who is in heaven' (Matt. 23.8–9). Is there anything in the fact that Luke's parable of the Good Samaritan uses a priest and a Levite as the antithesis to the one who was to serve Jesus' disciples as the model of the loving neighbour (Luke 10.29–37)? And in the case of the Fourth Gospel we may simply note what has been called 'the individualism of John', characterized by his extended metaphor of Christ the true vine, where each of the branches is rooted directly in the vine itself (John 15.1–10). The picture of Christian churches and congregations which flourished and grew in the first two generations of Christianity without thought or presence or activity of priest remains constant throughout the NT material.

(b) The Epistle to the Hebrews has the most to say on the subject of priesthood of any NT document and has justifiably been called 'the epistle of priesthood'. What it says is very striking. Basically it works with a double distinction: between the old age/covenant and the new (Jewish eschatology); and between the world of shadow/imperfection and the real/heavenly world (Platonism). It achieves its powerful effect by merging these two distinctions. The old age/covenant is the age of shadow/imperfection. The new age/covenant introduced by Christ is the age of fulfilment/reality. Judaism with its cult and institutions belongs to the old age of imperfection. The priesthood of Aaron, the tabernacle and the sacrificial system are all part of that imperfect shadow. But Christ has brought the age of shadow and imperfection to an end. He is the real priest, who by his death and ascension has opened the way into the real temple/presence of God in heaven, by offering the only real/really effective sacrifice (himself). The argument is somewhat strange to us today and to grasp its full sweep it is best to read chs. 5—10 as a whole (NEB appropriately heads these chapters 'The shadow and the real'). But the keynote is struck in such verses as 9.11–12, 23–4 and 10.1.

The point is that for the writer to the Hebrews there is only one who can now properly be called 'priest' – Jesus himself. His priesthood is of a unique kind: he qualifies for it by virtue of his resurrection ('by the power of an indestructible life', 7.16). No ordinary human being can match that type – 'the order of Melchizedek' (7.3). Moreover, by virtue of this one true priest's effective ministry all believers can now enter directly the very presence of God himself, without the mediation of human priests. Hence the writer's repeated exhortations to 'draw near' (4.16; 7.25; 10.22). Consequently those who yearn for a priesthood of the old kind, like the order of Aaron, are in danger of falling back into the era of shadow and imperfection and of losing the immediacy of that communion with God which it was Christ's whole purpose to bring about.

Here we may say a clear principle has been enunciated, albeit in the Letter's own distinctive terms. Christianity marks a break with Judaism precisely on this point of priesthood. For the author of Hebrews Christianity is different from Judaism precisely because it no longer has a priesthood set apart within the ranks of believers. The need for such mediation between God and his covenanted people was precisely what Jesus came to abolish. Previously the high priest was the only one who could enter God's presence in the holy of holies, and that only on the Day of Atonement. But now all believers can go direct to the presence of God by the direct mediation of Christ himself.

It has never failed to astonish me that a principle so clearly formulated could be so blatantly ignored or side-stepped by those who insist that nevertheless, despite Hebrews, an order of priesthood is necessary within Christianity. To use Hebrews 5.1 to justify or explain Christian priesthood, as Vatican II does,[3] while ignoring the thrust and argument of the Letter as a whole is a form of eisegesis which ranks more as abuse than as correct use of Scripture. Similarly the argument that the function of Christian priests is to represent the one true priesthood of Christ reads more like a rationalization than a justification. And since it interposes once again a mediator of grace between believer and God, when the concern of Hebrews was to convince his readers that such mediation was no longer necessary, it can hardly look for support to Hebrews in good faith. Mormons who operate with two orders of priesthood, the Aaronic and the Melchizedek, seem to have misunderstood the argument of the Letter still more. But the mistake is basically the same. What price the canonical authority of Hebrews when one of its principal concerns is treated so casually and twisted to serve a variation of the very case it was written to oppose?

(c) The Letter to the Hebrews is not alone on this point within the NT. On the contrary it is simply the clearest statement of a position which evidently characterized the first Christian communities and teachers. Fundamental was the conviction that Christ had introduced the new age and covenant of Jewish expectation. Part of that expectation had been the hope for an immediacy in knowing God and for the universality of prophetic inspiration (Isa. 54.13; Jer. 31.31–4; Joel 2.28–9). Christians were sure that these prophecies had been fulfilled in their experience (John 6.43–51; 2 Cor. 3.2–18; Acts 2.17–18). This is precisely why 1 Peter and Revelation in the passages already referred to above (a) can speak of all Christians as priests. Because they saw the ancient ideal of Israel as 'a kingdom of priests' and 'priests of the Lord' (Exod. 19.6; Isa. 61.6) now at last fulfilled in the movement which had sprung from Christ's ministry in life, death and resurrection. Christianity saw its distinction from Judaism precisely in that the limitation of priesthood and inspiration had been transcended. When Clement resorted once again to the distinction between 'priest' and 'laity' (1 Clem. 40.5), he was pointing down a road which would fundamentally compromise if not make a mere cypher of a very basic element in earliest Christianity's self-understanding.

It is no surprise that this concept of a universal priesthood of believers was bound up with Christianity's early sense of being the eschatological fulfilment of God's covenant purpose with

Israel. And no surprise that the dilution of the eschatological perspective was accompanied by the reassertion of a concept of limited priesthood. But it is now generally recognized that eschatology is an unavoidable feature of the NT writings. So once again the uncomfortable question arises: Is there an important aspect of the NT's definition of Christianity which has been lost sight of and whose loss deprives Christianity of one of its claims to distinctiveness within the purpose of God over against the earlier revelation of the OT?

The same point emerges from the occasional use of cultic language in other passages within the NT, in particular Paul's call to the Christians in Rome to 'present your bodies as a sacrifice to God, living, holy, acceptable, your spiritual worship' (Rom. 12.1). What is striking here is the use of sacrificial categories: Christians *should* offer sacrifice! But what is even more striking is the way in which he has taken the category wholly out of the cult. The sacrifice Christians are to offer is not of beast or bird on bloody altar, but the sacrifice of their lives in the ordinary physical involvement of everyday commerce and intercourse. The cult has been desacralized. Or, better, everyday life has been sanctified. The implications for priesthood are the same as before. If there is no sacrificial offering other than that of oneself then there is no role for a particular order of priests within the community of belief. Equally, if sacrifice constitutes the priest, and if each believer must offer himself or herself in sacrifice, then, once again, all believers are priests. Typical of the failure to see the force of this exhortation were some of the early statements regarding industrial chaplaincies, which seemed to imply that the Church was not present in industry unless and until an ordained clergyman became involved on the factory floor. On the contrary, if Paul is to be taken seriously, it was precisely the Christian layperson bearing witness by the quality of his or her work and relationships who was offering up the real Christian sacrifice, priestly mediator and representative of Christ and Church on the altar of everyday encounter. And it is precisely the failure to take such a text with canonical seriousness which underlies the weakness of the typical ecumenical statements about 'the ministry of the whole people of God'.

As a counter to such points reference is often made to Paul's description of his own ministry in priestly terms – 'a minister of Christ Jesus to the Gentiles in the priestly service of the gospel of God, so that the offering of the Gentiles may be acceptable, sanctified by the Holy Spirit' (Rom. 15.16). The argument is that Paul did, after all, think of himself as a priest, or at least in priestly terms; and so the more limited application of the concept of priestly ministry, and so of priesthood, is legitimated. But this is to miss the point. Paul does not regard his ministry to the Gentiles as distinctively priestly over against other Christian ministries such as all Christians are called to. The language used in Rom. 15.16 is simply a particular example of the language already used in 12.1. Paul's ministry to the Gentiles can be described in priestly terms because *all* Christian service in the new covenant can be so described. He speaks in the same way in Phil. 2.17, of his ministry to and for the Christians in Philippi. But evidently he thought of their ministry to him through Epaphroditus in similar terms (Phil. 2.25, 30), as also of the Gentile Christians' participation in the collection for the saints in Jerusalem (Rom. 15.26; 2 Cor. 9.12).

In each case the point remains the same: a distinctive feature of the earliest Christian self-understanding was the conviction that what had been possible and proper only in the temple and by means of the temple ritual was now to be enjoyed and practised throughout the eschatological people of God in their ministry of everyday vocation. The language and meaning of priestly ministry and sacrifice was not to be lost. But it was retained precisely by breaking down the barrier between cult and everyday life, between priest and laity. All could see their diverse ministries in priestly terms simply because priestly categories were no longer restricted to a particular order or group within the congregations of Christians. Here again we seem to be in touch with a fundamental stratum in earliest Christian self-definition.

It is the apparent disregard for something quite so fundamental by subsequent Christian history that does more to undermine the canonical authority of the New Testament than most heresies. Could it be that this is one of the most important underlying reasons why the issue of church order has proved so intractable in ecumenical discussions? Because the major authority acknowledged by all Christians (the NT) has been effectively discounted and ignored? Here certainly the dialogue of theology has to allow the NT to speak afresh and to have a more important say than has usually been the case hitherto.

2 EUCHARIST

As the previous chapter reminds us, *Lumen Gentium* is clear that there is a 'ministerial or hierarchical priesthood' which is different in essence and not only in degree from the 'holy and royal priesthood' of all believers. That difference lies in the 'sacred power' which the Christian priest has to offer (or re-present) the eucharistic sacrifice.[4] This tie-in between priesthood and sacrifice is hardly surprising. It had been fundamental to Judaism, as indeed to all religions of the time. And it was the reacceptance of the category of sacrifice as a continuing cultic obligation by influential figures in the post-apostolic churches which no doubt made the re-emergence of an order of priesthood within Christianity inevitable. Of course a sacrifice requires a priest to offer it. No one would think otherwise. It was by such acceptance of the normal assumptions of the time, such assimilation to 'the pattern of this age', we may say, that the eschatological perspective of the first Christians was lost and with it the distinctiveness of the NT concept of priesthood.

Nor is this concept of a priesthood 'different in essence' from the priesthood of the faithful confined to Roman Catholicism. Despite much trumpeting of the concept of 'the priesthood of all believers', most of the major Reformation traditions have retained it in fact. 'New Presbyter is but old Priest writ large' (Milton). The crucial factor being, once again, the fact that only ordained clergy may preside at the Eucharist. The word 'priest' may be shunned. The category of 'sacrifice' may be used only in an attenuated sense. But the fact that only the ordained minister can preside at Holy Communion means that it all comes to the same thing. The ordained clergyman (or clergyperson) is exercising a priesthood distinct in essence from the priesthood of all. It will not do to reply, as some do, that in principle any believer may act in this specially representative capacity, or that eucharistic presidency is reserved to the ordained primarily for the sake of good order. Until a 'layperson' presides at the Lord's Supper when (other) ordained ministers are present, it cannot be denied that ordained ministry is, at this central point at least, different in essence from the ministry of the whole people of God. Like it or not, most Christian denominations function with an order of priesthood different in essence from the priesthood of all believers, and that by virtue of the fact that only the priest can administer the sacrament which is the chief means of grace for most Christians. What does the dialogue with the NT say on this subject?

(a) It is obvious that the memory of Jesus' Last Supper with his disciples was cherished by the first Christians. Each of the first three Gospels recalls the scene with care and with specific reminder of the words spoken by Jesus over the bread and over the cup of wine (Matt. 26.26–8; Mark 14.22–4; Luke 22.19–20). Indication is clearly given that special significance was intended by these symbols – Christ's body broken, the blood of the (new) covenant poured out for many. The importance is confirmed by the account preserved in 1 Corinthians 11, a tradition which Paul explicitly states was handed on by him to the new Corinthian congregation, and, by implication to all the churches he established. It is with Paul that the command, 'Do this in remembrance of me', is explicitly attached to the words over both bread and cup (1 Cor. 11.24–5). And though the command is not present, or uniformly present in the Gospels, the implication there is the same: the accounts were preserved because they were living tradition within the churches. The words over bread and wine were being regularly said in repeated representations of the Lord's Supper.

So, despite the silence on the subject elsewhere in the NT it can hardly be doubted that the breaking of bread and drinking of wine in remembrance of Christ was an established feature of the Christian churches from the first, and regarded as a matter of first importance in their common life – a means of sharing in the Body and Blood of Christ (1 Cor 10.16) and so of sharing in the fruits of the new covenant which he had established by his death and resurrection. The probable use of eucharistic terminology in John 6 may be regarded as sufficient confirmation – 'unless you eat the flesh of the Son of Man and drink his blood, you have no life in you' (John 6.53). But the cautionary corollary

needs to be added that John seems to be using the language of
eating and drinking as images of coming to and believing in
Christ (6.29, 35, 37, 40, 44, 45, 47), and that he takes some care
lest the talk of eating Christ's flesh be understood in too literal
a way – 'It is the Spirit that gives life, the flesh is of no avail'
(6.63).

But if the Lord's Supper is shown thus to have been important
across the spectrum of first-century Christianity, what does that
say about the link between Eucharist and priest? Does the NT
give any support to the subsequent idea of a priesthood distinctive by virtue of its sacred power to make participation in the
Body and Blood of Christ possible for the faithful? Since there
is no thought of a ministerial priesthood within the NT, as we
have seen above, such a conception of the Eucharist is hardly
likely to be grounded there either. But in addition there are
other features of what the NT writers say in relation to this
subject which need to be heard in the dialogue of theology.

(b) One is the setting of the eucharistic elements within the
context of a shared meal. This is indicated by the way in which
the Gospels present the Last Supper as a reinterpretation of the
Jewish Passover. There bread and cup were part of the larger
meal. The words said by Jesus would have come at separate
parts of the meal. The cup which Jesus interpreted as symbol of
the new covenant would have been one of four cups of wine
drunk at different points within the whole. Although special
significance was being given to these two elements within the
meal the context of the meal remained important. The bread
and the wine were being used to give a new understanding of the
meal as a whole and to the community who celebrated it. The
fellowship reality of the new covenant was to be expressed in a
common meal whose significance came to focus in the words
spoken by Jesus over the bread and one of the cups.

Seeing the Last Supper in this light helps bring home an
important aspect of it too much neglected in subsequent eucharistic theology – the fact that the Last Supper was the last of
the fellowship meals which were a particular characteristic of
Jesus' ministry. During his ministry Jesus was often a guest at
meals (e.g. Mark 1.29–31; Luke 7.36; 14.1; John 2.1–11), and
at least on some occasions he evidently did his own entertaining

(Mark 2.15–17; Luke 15.1–2; and not forgetting Mark 6.30–44 and 8.1–9). Indeed his table habits and the character of his table-fellowship became something of a byword and scandal – 'a glutton and a drunkard, a friend of tax-collectors and sinners' (Matt. 11.19). Equally significant was the eschatological significance with which he invested them. So far as Jesus was concerned, to share in table-fellowship with him was a symbol and anticipation of the messianic banquet of the age to come (e.g. Mark 2.19; Matt. 22.1–10/Luke 14.16–24; Luke 22.30). As with the Last Supper in particular, the hope of the new covenant community was expressed, and to some extent at least, realized in the fellowship of the common meal.

The point is further borne out in the accounts of the resurrection appearances and of the early Church and mission in Acts. The risen Jesus revealed himself in the breaking of bread and the sharing of food (Luke 24.30–1, 41–3; John 21.13; Acts 1.4), that is in actions which had characterized his fellowship with them prior to his death. So too the earliest Christian community in Jerusalem continued the same practice, breaking bread in each other's homes and sharing food (Acts 2.42, 46). Whether Luke intends by 'breaking bread' a particular reference to (one of) the eucharistic elements as such is disputed Probably not, since in Acts 20.7 and 11 he describes two breakings of bread within a few hours of each other. And in 27.34–6 'breaking of bread' obviously refers to a hurried meal taken to keep up the strength of the boat's passengers and crew in a situation of long sustained crisis. But since the words of the Last Supper were being preserved and used throughout this period, as we must suppose, it is equally probably that at least some of these passages *include* a reference to the eucharistic elements. Or, more precisely, it must be judged probable that some at least of the meals shared in common by the earliest Christian congregations included the recollection of the words of the Last Supper as part of them, possibly as a christianized passover, or more regularly 'on the first day of the week' (Acts 20.7).

This seems to be further confirmed by Paul's treatment in 1 Cor. 10 and 11. The Lord's Supper continues to be understood as a fellowship meal. This can be seen from the fact that Paul draws a triple comparison between the sacrificial meal in Israel's cult (Lev. 7.6, 15), the feast in a pagan temple and the Lord's Supper itself (10.18-22). And in 11.17-34 the bread and the wine are clearly thought of in the context of the common meal, with the bread being eaten at some point within the meal and as part of it and the wine drunk 'after supper' (11.25). Moreover in 10.16-21 the emphasis is precisely on fellowship, common participation in the blood and body of Christ (*koinonia* and *koinonos* occur four times in vv.16-20), partaking together from the same loaf, the same table (vv.17, 21). This is precisely why it is so difficult to be sure whether, when Paul warns against failure to 'discern the body' (11.29), he is referring to the eucharistic bread (cf. 10.16; 11.24) or to the Christian congregation (cf. 10.17; 12.27). Precisely because Paul has in view the common life of the congregation, created by the Spirit (12.13), sustained in and expressed by the common meal (11.20-2, 33-4) and particularly the sharing in bread and wine together, 'in remembrance of him'.

Given the consistent prominence of table-fellowship and of the common meal as the context of the Lord's Supper within the NT it needs to be considered whether the separation of the Eucharist into a ritual act on its own has lost something of major importance in the experience and practice of Christian community. Of course justification can be readily found for the separation. In particular, the setting of bread and wine in close parallel in Mark 14.22-4 and 1 Cor. 10.16 may seem to have invited holding them together in separate acts clearly distinct from, or at least within, the meal as a whole. But the growing tendency in the post-apostolic churches to see them in terms of a sacrifice offered by a priest (even if in 'concelebration' by the whole community – Schillebeeckx) must have consolidated the trend and made it irreversible. Here again the loss of the eschatological perspective characteristic of Jesus and the first Christians and the beginning of the re-emergence of an order of priesthood seem to go hand in hand and to mark the loss of a dimension of fellowship, common participation which was a central feature of Christian beginnings. There is a question here about the contrast between Jesus' table-fellowship as a 'foretaste of the heavenly banquet' and the traditional eucharistic practice to which the same phrase has been attached. And in the ecumenical dialogue with the NT that question should not be ignored.

(c) Other points may be mentioned more briefly. One is the fact that the words of the Last Supper are passed down to us in different forms.

Matt. – Take, eat; this is my body
Mark – Take;   this is my body
Luke –   This is my body which is given for you
Paul –   This is my body which is broken for you
John – The bread which I...give...is my flesh

Matt. – This is my blood of the covenant, which is poured out for many for the forgiveness of sins
Mark – This is my blood of the covenant, which is poured out for many
Luke – This cup which is poured out for you is the new covenant in my blood
Paul – This cup is the new covenant in my blood. Do this, as often as you drink it, in remembrance of me
John – My blood is drink indeed

From this, and the fact that no attempt was made to preserve Jesus' words in Aramaic (as the first Christians preserved *abba* and *maranatha* – Rom. 8.15; I Cor. 16.22), we may deduce that the words were not remembered as a sacred formula whose significance (and power) depended on their being said in a particular form. Like the rest of the Jesus tradition they were remembered as living tradition whose substance was retained but whose form could vary according to context and speaker.

Add to this the fact that there was no such thing as a 'sacred space' for these first Christians. As already noted, the distinction between cult and common, sacred and secular, was one which they believed to have been left behind in the old age. With Christ's resurrection they had moved into a new age where disputes about sacred sites were now irrelevant (John 4.19–24). The only temple which mattered now was the risen Christ in whom they must abide (John 2.19–21; 15), or the temple of the Christian indwelt by the Spirit (I Cor. 3.16–17), or the temple consisting of the Christian community itself (I Pet. 2.5). What this meant in practice is that the first Christian congregations met in homes – home churches. In these circumstances the context of the Eucharist was likely to be the meal table in the home. And the host was most likely to be the householder, whose guests the little congregation were – Prisca and Aquila (Rom. 16.5; 1 Cor. 16.19), Nympha (Col. 4.15) and Philemon (Philem. 2) – two of those named being women, we may note. There is nothing in any of our texts to counter the most obvious implication: that when the Lord's Supper was celebrated, it would have been the host(ess) who in the course of the common meal reminded his or her guests of the words first said by Jesus on the night on which he was betrayed. The whole thrust of our canonical traditions points away from any suggestion that presiding on such occasions was reserved for a special group within the churches or that the speaking of the 'words of institution' was some sort of priestly prerogative. Insofar as continuity of tradition and universality of practice were already seen as important, they were evidently provided by the words spoken, not by the person or status of the one who spoke them.

Finally, a comment may be in order about the understanding of the Eucharist as one of the chief 'means of grace', if not the means of grace *par excellence*. Certainly if one is to take 1 Cor. 10.16–17 seriously one is bound to rank the Eucharist highly as a 'means of grace'. And the Reformed emphasis on the Word of God as also sacrament and necessarily to be conjoined to the sacrament for it to be efficacious is an important qualification. Even so it is clear that reserving the Lord's Supper to priestly prerogative has been at the heart of clerical power down through the centuries. By being able to withhold the sacrament of the Body and Blood of Christ priests could threaten to deny other believers access to divine grace.

What seems to have been almost wholly forgotten here is Paul's teaching on grace, the most explicit and full exposition of the subject in the NT. In particular his understanding of charism (*charisma*) which is derived from the Greek for 'grace' (*charis*). For charism means 'manifestation or embodiment of grace' and refers to any word or action by which grace is ministered to the Body of Christ (Rom. 12.4–8; 1 Cor. 12; Eph. 4.7–16; 1 Pet. 4.10–11). And that is just the point. *Charisma* is actually the closest Greek we have to the phrase 'means of grace'. And it refers to a wide range of ministry. Moreover, as the passages just referred to make clear, *each* believer should see her/himself as such a minister of grace (every Christian a 'charismatic' in the proper sense of the term). In other words, to limit the 'means of grace' so drastically as has traditionally been the case within Christianity, to confine the ministers of grace in ecclesiology and *de facto* praxis to priest and ordained clergy, and to focus so narrowly on the Eucharist administered by priest as the means of grace without which all other means of grace become meaningless, has meant an impoverishment of doctrine and in the realization of grace of incalculable proportions. Here certainly the canonical texts must be allowed to speak with a fresh voice and in so speaking (and being heard?!) may hope to contribute not only to the ongoing dialogue of theology but to a rekindling of a renewed ecumenical vision.

3   ORDINATION

Integrally bound up with the two preceding subjects is, of course, the issue of ordination. For it is by ordination that the peculiar power of the priest to officiate at the Eucharist is restricted and controlled. If there is an 'essential difference' between clergy and laity, it is ordination which gives it. Moreover, at a time when fresh thought is being given to the overall pattern of ministry, and particularly to the theology and character of diaconal ministry, and to the ordination of women within Anglican and Catholic ministry, the meaning and function of ordination is certainly central to the discussion. Consequently even our brief treatment would be incomplete without some mention of ordination within the dialogue of NT theology.

(a) There is certainly a concept and practice of ordination within the NT. Jesus 'appointed twelve that they might be with him and that he might send them out to preach' (Mark 3.14). The earliest Jerusalem church chose seven men whom the apostles appointed to administer the common fund by the laying on of hands (Acts 6.3–6). Barnabas and Saul were commissioned by the prophets and teachers who led the church in Antioch by the laying on of their hands (Acts 13.3). And in 1 Tim. 4.14 and 2 Tim. 1.6 there is a clear concept of ordination (of Timothy):

'Do not neglect the spiritual gift in you which was given through
prophecy, with the laying on of hands of the elders as a body';
'Stir up the gift of God which is in you through the laying on
of my hands'. We certainly do not need to wait, therefore, for
a Clement or an Ignatius or a Hippolytus for the concept of
ordained ministry.

(b) However, this conclusion must be integrated into our earlier
findings. For in the light of these findings, what is in mind in
such NT passages cannot be the same understanding of ordination as that which constitutes a priest and marks off one form
of ministry as 'essentially different' from all other ministry. On
the contrary, the NT precedents for ordination are not confined
to one kind of pattern (far less 'order') of ministry. Consequently it may legitimately be asked from the NT side of the
dialogue whether any concept of ordination which divides
Christian ministry into two distinct kinds can be justified in
terms of the NT. This point can be documented fairly readily.

According to our sources the commissionings which determined the emergence and growth of the Christian Church as
such were made by the risen Christ. In Matthew it would
appear that it was only the eleven who received 'the great
commission' (Matt. 28.16–20). But in Luke it is clearly implied
that the eleven together with 'the rest of the company' are in
view (Luke 24.33–53). Likewise in Acts it seems to be the whole
company of disciples, some 120 in all, who are promised the
commissioning and empowering Spirit, and who in the event
receive the outpoured Spirit on the day of Pentecost, fulfilling
Joel's prophecy of a widespread outpouring of the Spirit 'in the
last days' (Acts 1—2; particularly 1.15; 2.16–18). Similarly, in
the equivalent passages in the Fourth Gospel, John seems to
take care to speak of those who received the Spirit and the
commissioning simply as 'the disciples', representative of all
disciples (John 20.19–23).

It is not finally clear how all these passages are to be integrated
and how they advance the discussion of ordination – not least
since none of them says anything about a laying on of hands.
Certainly they point to the reality of a distinct ministry of
apostleship – those commissioned by the risen Christ to preach
the gospel and establish churches (1 Cor. 9.1–2; Gal. 2.8). But

that was also understood as a unique ministry, a closed circle
into which Paul just squeezed 'last of all' (1 Cor. 15.8; cf. Acts
1.21–2), belonging to the founding period of Christianity (Eph.
2.20), last act on the stage of world history (1 Cor. 4.9). But they
also indicate that commissioning to serve as witnesses to Christ
was part of the 'package' of receiving the Spirit. So that we are
not surprised that a Philip who was appointed to wait on tables
proved to be a very effective evangelist (Acts 8). Nor that the
decisive breakthrough at Antioch was the work of unknown and
'ordinary' believers (Acts 11.19–21). Likewise the conversion
and commissioning of Paul (for that is how Paul always thinks
of it) was at the hands of the otherwise unknown Ananias (Acts
9.17; 22.12–16). And the 'updating' of Apollos, another whom
Paul seems to call 'apostle' (1 Cor. 4.9), was the work of Priscilla
and Aquila (Acts 18.24–6). So it would be difficult to draw any
tight concept of ordination, let alone of apostolic succession,
from all these passages.

In fact we seem to come closer to a more consistently NT
conception of ordination if we think of conversion and initiation
in terms of ordination. This is the implication of the very dynamic picture of the Spirit's coming upon enquirers and initiates
in Acts – acceptance by God as a being baptized in the Spirit for
witness (Acts 1.8; 11.15–17). Paul's conception of initiation into
the Body of Christ is of a similarly dynamic character (1 Cor.
12.13 in context): to be a member of the Body of Christ is to
have a function as an organ of the body; to have received grace
(*charis*) is to become a channel (or means) of grace to others
(*charisma*). John's conception of the believer as Spirit-endowed is
equally vigorous: enabled by the Spirit to offer true worship
(John 4.24); as having the Spirit's anointing, and so not needing
anyone else to mediate teaching (1 John 2.27).

If the NT is to be allowed to speak in a theological and
ecclesiological dialogue about ordination, therefore, it needs to
be given a hearing on two points: the fundamental ordination is
the gift of the Spirit to all who believe; and the diversities of
ministry which ensue are no different in kind from one another.

(c) When we look at the 'ordination passages' themselves more
closely a further aspect becomes evident. Certainly the passages
referred to in (a) have in view particular ministries – that is,

specific ministries within the general obligation to ministry which lies upon all believers. But what is striking here is the number of these specific ministries which were short-term. Philip did not regard his commissioning to wait on tables as a life-long commission, or assume that he needed a further or different commission before he took the gospel to the Samaritans (Acts 8). The commissioning of Barnabas and Saul described in Acts 13.3 was evidently understood as their being set apart by the church at Antioch as missionaries of that church – a commissioning in effect for the first missionary journey (so that 'apostles' in Acts 14.4, 14 probably means simply emissaries of Antioch); certainly when Paul thinks of his commissioning as apostle to the Gentiles he never looks beyond the commissioning received at his conversion (1 Cor. 15.8–11; Gal. 1.1, 11–12, 15–17). Elsewhere in Paul the point is much the same. 2 Cor. 8.19 uses a verb which perhaps comes closer than any other to the sense 'ordain'. But it refers to the appointment of a brother by his local church to assist Paul in the matter of the collection which Paul was making for the poor Christians in Jerusalem. An appointment once again limited in time and scope – a short-term ordination. And 1 Cor. 16.15 speaks of Stephanas and his household having appointed themselves to a particular ministry.

It is certainly true, as we have seen, that the Pastoral Epistles seem to envisage a more developed concept of ministry and a more developed form of ordination. But the Pastorals are not the only NT voice on the matter. And if we are looking for NT principles and precedents, it would seem equally clear that there is much to be said for a broader concept of ordination and for different kinds of ordination, and much against the traditional concepts of priestly ministry and ordination. To begin to categorize grace into different classes, qualitatively different in character and effectiveness, is a fearful step for a follower of Jesus to take. And to begin to narrow the channels of grace in the way in which the classical theory of ordination does, seems to be an attempt to recreate the very form of religion which Jesus and the NT writers seem to have been reacting against and to have rejoiced at leaving behind in their sense of eschatological fulfilment. Is this an over-reaction? That can only become clear if the dialogue of NT theology is allowed to proceed with the NT allowed to speak in its own terms and with its own concerns.

CONCLUSION

This chapter has clearly been the view of one NT theologian, and idiosyncratic some may no doubt find it. But it is put forward as one example of how long-standing debates and issues might look from a NT perspective if the texts could be allowed to speak in their own terms without the filter of denominational tradition and centuries-old vested interest. The fact that similar questions can be raised from the side of systematic theology (Chapter 5) is at least some confirmation that there are questions to be asked on these issues, questions which cannot be dismissed as an unrealistic attempt to extricate the NT from the tradition of the Church.

NOTES

1 I have in mind particularly the Second Vatican Council's Document on the Church (*Lumen Gentium*), the two statements on Ministry by the Anglican-Roman Catholic International Commission (1973 and 1979), the World Council of Churches' Lima text, *Baptism Eucharist and Ministry* (1982), and the Faith and Order report on this theme to the British Methodist Conference in 1986.
2 But note the very important thesis of Schillebeeckx to which J. M. refers in Chapter 5.
3 See Chapter 5 above.
4 *Lumen Gentium* 10.

Epilogue

The fact is that Christianity is bound to look back to its foundation period for guidelines and principles in its theologizing. For the doctrine of the incarnation carries with it the inevitable corollary that the fullest and clearest manifestation of the divine character and will was expressed in a particular person and history. There is therefore an inescapable obligation laid upon Christians continually to look back to that period and to that person in history in order to measure their faith and practice against the revelation which they believe is there contained.

In the documents which now comprise the New Testament and which have been preserved from the beginning, the Christian community has traditionally recognized the earliest and most authoritative witness to that revelation of God in Jesus the Christ. Hence the task of measuring faith and practice against the original revelation inevitably entails recourse to the New Testament as the supreme criterion of orthodoxy and orthopraxis.

Of course the New Testament documents need to be interpreted, and the tradition of the Church could be said to provide that interpretation. But such a simple formula, if left unanalysed, can lead the unwary into a veritable minefield. Will some be tempted to limit interpretation to the traditions adopted within their own Christian denomination, or to use these as the set criteria for judging all other denominations? Will they then reduce the rich diversity of New Testament imagery and thought to their traditions of faith and practice? Even if they prove to be more truly ecumenical and to respect the equal rights of other denominational traditions of faith and practice, will they reduce the rich variety of New Testament imagery and thought to the full breadth of the stream of Christian tradition of faith and practice? Even then how will they deal with matters which to this day prove to be so contentious between the Christian denominations? And will they ever be able to see how much of the cultures through which Christianity has passed in the course of two millennia, has entered – already in New Testament times – into its various understandings of itself and into its developing structures and practices?

There has been much speculation in modern times about the impossibility of presuppositionless judgement, and in the case of the quest for authoritative Christian origins this has taken the form of cautionary tales about never being able to get into the minds of the biblical authors, not to speak of getting behind these to the historical Jesus. More positively the point has been put that the past can only emerge at all for us, and the present can only come explicitly to consciousness, in the course of what has been called the merging of horizons of past and present, as we come with all the presuppositions of contemporary culture to a set of documents which, we must keep reminding ourselves, survive from an entirely different age. We have both accepted this general view of the matter, but we believe that the merging of horizons will only work as it should, and have the desired beneficial effects for our faith, if we pay the closest critical attention to the specific cultural categories of each horizon in the very process of 'merging' them; and this is where division of labour combined with close collaboration between scripture scholar and systematician can promise the best results. For the theologian who aspires also to be a teacher in the church there is always an inescapable tension in this merging of horizons in the study of the NT. For the NT comes to him with the strangeness and otherness of a far distant age and culture, and that strangeness constantly catches him by surprise as he researches a particular point or issue which outruns or challenges his starting point or assumptions. Moreover, though he comes to the NT as the earliest church tradition, he can never forget that Christianity began as a renewal movement, a movement of the Spirit which broke through the traditions and boundaries of earlier revelation, and an eschatological movement which was experienced as a liberation from humanly accumulated constraints on faith and worship. And it is that character of

Christianity as such renewal which has been preserved and enshrined in the pages of the NT Scriptures. To 'do' NT theology properly, therefore, will always have that potential for critical interaction with the traditions of the period, for renewal and liberation into fresh insights and patterns of faith and worship. And an inescapable obligation on the NT scholar as Christian teacher will be the harnessing and to some extent channelling of that potential.

So in the case of Christology, (s)he must be ready to call attention to those aspects of the scriptural tradition which have been set aside or played down in subsequent theology. Without disputing the importance of classical emphases drawn from the NT, the NT theologian nevertheless has to ask whether the neglect of some of these other emphases has in fact narrowed the understanding of God's revelation through Christ, has narrowed that revelation precisely by the insistence on a consistency of human logic which can be maintained only by that neglect, precisely by trying to contain the mystery of God's self-revelation in Jesus within a form of words, when the very point which the first Christians made over against their Jewish co-religionists was that God had revealed himself definitively in a human person and not in a written text.

Likewise with Christian ministry. In historical terms the renewal movement which was Christianity in the beginning was understood as the eschatological realization of the immediacy in divine-human relationships for which Old Testament prophets had longed without need of priest, as the direct knowledge of God's will without needing necessarily to depend on a human teacher. And though in the natural social evolution of human institutions Christianity soon developed its own firmer structures, and the 'routinizing of charisma' saw the re-emergence of a distinction between clergy and laity, the fact remains that the NT documents enshrine as a stronger emphasis the eschatological ideal. Inevitably then, here too it is part of the task of the NT scholar who values the NT also as canon to draw attention to the early ideal as well as the subsequent reality, to pose the question whether the evolving structures of the Church and the hopes of the ecumenical movement are paying sufficient heed to the ideal and to the diversity of charisms as constitutive of the unity of the Body of Christ.

When the perspective is broadened to include the varying traditions which Christians have developed in post-biblical times, it becomes necessary to pay particular attention to a further two features of these traditions if the authority of the original revelation is ever to come through to us today. First, to the common cultural categories which the Christians of successive ages have absorbed in the very process of creating their doctrines, rituals, codes and institutions. Second, to the manner in which the warring of divided Christian communities has itself created and perpetuated prejudices about the absolute validity of forms of doctrine, ritual, code and institution which particular traditions wished to maintain to the exclusion, rather than the enrichment, of others.

In the case of Christology it became clear that followers of Jesus from the beginning had borrowed religious images and concepts from existing cultures in order to express their claims for Jesus *vis-à-vis* divinity, in view of their experience of the revelation to humankind which they believed had come in him. Long before our time, however, it had become all too common in all Christian traditions to use these borrowed images and concepts of God's word and wisdom so as to issue exclusivist claims on behalf of Christianity or, at the very least, to make a pre-emptive strike for superiority, despite the fact that other religions used, and still use, just these images and concepts in order to point to other instances of divine revelation. It was not our intention to compose a contemporary Christology or to preclude other treatments of central christological themes in this series. But we could claim, in a combination of chapters which merge the horizons of Scripture and tradition while treating each with full critical respect, to have shown how Christology can liberate us from attitudes of exclusivism and superiority, and free us for commitment to the cause of Jesus in the service of God, in openness and service to all humankind.

Now just as certain interpretations of christological themes from Scripture and tradition place barriers between us and other religions of the race, so the development of forms of Christian ministry have set up barriers within the Christian community in the world, barriers that divide clergy from laity, and Christian denomination from Christian denomination. And these, once again, are not the natural divisions one can always find between varying developments which in their very variety serve to enrich each other and to produce unity without uniformity; they are, on the contrary, the crippling divisions that derive from claims which embody once more attitudes of exclusivism or, at the very least, superiority. It was highly significant to note how in the long development of forms of Christian ministry the logic of the factor which Roman Catholic theology calls the power of jurisdiction, gradually imposed its terms upon factors more central to the specific genius of ministry after the manner of Jesus. The *immediate* access for all to divine grace which Jesus opened up was narrowed, and in the case of such a central means of grace as Eucharist, closed to the laity, the *laos*, the people of God.

As in the case of Christology it was not our intention to provide a contemporary theology of ministry for any Christian Church, or for all of them, or to preclude other efforts to address such problems in the course of this series. But, as in the case of Christology, we hope to have shown how a constructively critical and co-operative merging of the horizons of Scripture and tradition can open Christian eyes to the great variety of forms which Christian ministry can legitimately take so that, as long as the specific Spirit which shaped the ministry of Jesus in his life and death inspires them all, they may be mutually enriching rather than communally divisive.

The original revelation for Christians took the form of a 'way', the life of a man and the death in which that life found its proper consummation. Now life, of its nature, can only continue by adapting and assimilating, by growing and changing. The followers of Jesus must live out the Spirit of Jesus in the changing circumstances of each age, in order that the Body of Christ may continue its redemptive mission in the world. Forms of doctrine, ritual, code and institution are essential to this life moving through history, but none of them can replace it or even constrain it to any of their passing shapes. We are therefore entitled to hope that we can generalize from the concrete examples we have used in this opening volume, and look forward to a series of books in which this same merging of horizons can continue to help liberate the Spirit originally incarnate in Jesus from the rigidity, exclusivism and authoritarianism which Christians of all denominations have all too frequently imposed upon it.

Further Reading

Chapter 1: The Task of New Testament Theology

Dunn, J. D. G. "Levels of Canonical Authority." *Horizons in Biblical Theology* 4, 1982.

A contribution to the discussion of "canonical criticism" begun by J. A. Sanders and B. Childs.

Hahn, Ferdinand. *Historical Investigation and New Testament Faith.* Philadelphia: Fortress Press, 1983.

A positive and balanced treatment.

Käsemann, Ernst. "The Problem of a New Testament Theology." *New Testament Studies* 19, 1972–73.

As sharp a posing of the problem as you will find by one of Bultmann's leading pupils, who devoted most of his scholarly career to work in this area.

Stuhlmacher, Peter. *Historical Criticism and Theological Interpretation of Scripture.* Philadelphia: Fortress Press, 1977.

A valuable overview by one who has done most to revive biblical theology as a viable concept and task.

Thiselton, Anthony C. *The Two Horizons.* Grand Rapids: Wm. B. Eerdmans Publishing Co., 1979.

A detailed and definitive treatment of an often off-puttingly complex subject.

Chapter 2: The Task of Systematic Theology

Grant, Robert M. *Gods and the One God.* Philadelphia: Westminster Press, 1986.

Contains in well-written and easily digested form a wealth of detail of the religious and social world in which Christianity had first to make its way; a world long past, to which Christianity had to adapt itself or adapt that world to it.

Mackey, James P. *The Christian Experience of God as Trinity.* New York: Crossroad Publishing Co., 1983.

A more specialized account of how Christians developed their unique doctrine of God (as Trinity) in conversation and controversy with early Greek pagan theologians; containing an account of the development of Greek pagan trinities.

———. *Modern Theology: A Sense of Direction.* New York: Oxford University Press, 1987.

A complimentary account of very different philosophies which in modern times are the dialogue partners or critics with which Christian faith now has to deal and which will shape it as inevitably as earlier dialogues did, but differently.

Wiles, M. F. *What Is Theology?* New York: Oxford University Press, 1977.

An authoritative introduction to the subject for intelligent and reasonably well-read beginners.

Chapter 3: Christology—A View from New Testament Theology

Brown, Raymond E. *Biblical Exegesis and Church Doctrine.* Mahwah, N.J.: Paulist Press, 1985.

———. *The Birth of the Messiah.* Garden City, N.Y.: Doubleday & Co., 1977.

All Brown's writings, the more popular no less than the academic, make an invaluable contribution to the dialogue between scholarship, faith, and tradition.

Dunn, J. D. G. *Christology in the Making.* Philadelphia: Westminster Press, 1980.

An attempt to trace the emergence of the doctrine of the incarnation.

FURHER READING   149

———. *The Evidence for Jesus.* Philadelphia: Westminster Press, 1986.

Popular lectures aimed at bridging the gap between lectern and pew and showing how scholarship can make an important contribution to clarifying the New Testament and the beginnings of Christianity for all levels of faith.

Jewett, Robert, ed. *Christology and Exegesis: New Approaches.* Semeia 30, 1984.

A range of contributions on recent discussion and new approaches in the study of New Testament Christology.

Chapter 4: Christology—A View from Systematic Theology

Hick, John. *Problems of Religious Pluralism.* New York: St. Martin's Press, 1985.

One of the many books John Hick has written in an effort to rethink Christianity's position in a religiously pluralist world.

Küng, Hans. *On Being a Christian.* Garden City, N.Y.: Doubleday & Co., 1976.

One of the most popular and influential accounts in recent years of what it means to follow Jesus, avoid Christian distortions of his message, and enlighten—rather than threaten—other religious and humanist philosophies.

Lampe, G. W. *God as Spirit.* New York: Oxford University Press, 1977.

The most thoroughgoing modern theological reinstatement of the concept of "Spirit" as a means of understanding God's creative and recreative activity, and especially God's presence in the world in Jesus. Slightly spoiled by a prejudice against the corresponding concept of "Word."

Mackey, James P. *Jesus, the Man and the Myth.* New York: Paulist Press, 1979.

An example of one of the many contemporary efforts to assess the quest of the historical Jesus and his relationship to the Christ his followers have worshiped through the ages.

Pannenberg, Wolfhart, ed. *Revelation as History.* New York: Macmillan Co., 1968.

An important stage on the road taken by the modern theology of revelation as it sought to prove that divine revelation takes the form of historical events rather than divine dictation.

Chapter 5: Church Ministry—A View from Systematic Theology

Bouyer, Louis. *Eucharist.* Notre Dame, Ind.: University of Notre Dame Press, 1968.

A user-friendly account of the scriptural, historical, and theological data for a contemporary understanding of this central Christian sacrament.

Brown, Raymond E. *Priest and Bishop.* New York: Paulist/Newman Press, 1970.

A New Testament scholar investigates the origins of these offices, and some of the differences between them, in the many New Testament texts and contexts that deal with early Christian ministry.

Küng, Hans. *Structures of the Church.* New York: Crossroad Publishing Co., 1982.

Not at all user-friendly, but the kind of detailed and complex account of historical models and movements that alone can allow a modern person to understand how major offices and institutions in the Roman Catholic Church gradually became what they are today.

McKenna, J. H. *Eucharist and Holy Spirit.* Alcuin Club Collections 57. Great Wakering: Mayhew-McCrimmon, 1975.

Schillebeeckx, Edward. *The Church with a Human Face.* New York: Crossroad Publishing Co., 1985.

Chapter 6: Church Ministry—A View from New Testament Theology

Banks, Robert. *Paul's Idea of Community.* Grand Rapids: Wm. B. Eerdmans Publishing Co., 1980.

A readable and valuable treatment, drawing out the significance of the fact that Christian churches began meeting in private houses.

Barrett, C. K. *Church, Ministry, and Sacraments in the New Testament.* Grand Rapids: Wm. B. Eerdmans Publishing Co., 1985.

Nontechnical lectures setting out the mature understanding of one of the greatest of New Testament exegetes alive today.

Dunn, J. D. G. *Jesus and the Spirit.* Philadelphia: Westminster Press, 1975.

A study of the religious experience of the first Christians, including its corporate dimensions and implications.

Harvey, Anthony E. *Priest or President?* London: SPCK, 1975.

An Anglican contribution questioning, among other things, whether presidency of the Eucharist need be confined always to the priestly ordained.

Perkins, Pheme. *Ministering in the Pauline Churches.* Ramsey, N.J.: Paulist Press, 1982.

Popular lectures that include reflection on women in worship and ministry.

Schweizer, Eduard. *Church Order in the New Testament.* Naperville, Ill.: Alec R. Allenson, 1961.

An important contribution by the great Swiss scholar demonstrating the range and diversity of church order and ministry in earliest Christianity.

Index of Biblical References

Genesis
16.7-13 69
17.17 68

Exodus
19.6 126

Leviticus
7.6 133
7.15 133

Numbers
22–24 67
24.17 67

Deuteronomy
6.4 75

Judges
13.3-5 69

Job
1–2 75
28 76

Psalms
85.10-11 58
104.24 56

Proverbs
2.6 58
3.19 56
8.22 56
8.25 56
8.26-27 57

Isaiah
7.14 65, 66
51.9 58
54.13 126
61.6 126

Jeremiah
31.31-34 126

Joel
2.28-29 126

Wisdom
7.24 76
7.26 56
8.5 56
8.21–9.2 58
10–11 58

Ecclesiasticus
1.1 58
1.4 57
18.1-4 58
24.9 57
24.23 62, 76
43.26 57

Baruch
3 76
4.1 62, 76

2 Maccabees
6.2 75

Matthew
1–2 65, 71
1.20 65
1.23 65
5.17-20 10
11.19 132
22.1-10 132
22.16 73
23.8-9 124
26.26-28 130
28.16-20 137

Mark
1.29-31 131
2.15-17 132
2.19 132
3.14 136
3.31-35 68
6.3 68
6.30-44 132
7.19 10
8.1-9 132

12.14 73
14.22-24 130, 133

Luke
1–2 65-71
1.11-20 69
1.18 69
1.32-35 65
7.36 131
10.29-37 124
14.1 131
14.16-24 132
15.1-2 132
18.22 6
20.21 73
22.19-20 130
22.30 132
24.30-31 132
24.33-53 137
24.41-43 132

John
1.1-18 76
1.5 77-78
1.9 78
1.14 78
1.17 76
2.1-11 131
2.3-4 68
2.15 134
2.19-21 134
3.19-21 77
4.19-24 134
5.24 77
6.29 131
6.35 72, 131
6.37 131
6.38 72
6.40 131
6.43-51 126
6.44 131
6.45 131

Index of Names and Subjects

DATE DUE

Demco, Inc. 38-293